DATE DUE

Institutions in Modern America

INSTITUTIONS IN MODERN AMERICA

INNOVATION IN STRUCTURE AND PROCESS

Edited by Stephen E. Ambrose

The Johns Hopkins Press Baltimore

Baltimore, Maryland 21218

Printed in the United States of America

Library of Congress Catalog Card No. 67-16043

THE CONTRIBUTORS

David Brody, associate professor of history at Ohio State University, was born on June 5, 1930. He received his A.B. in 1952, his M.A. in 1953, and his Ph.D. in 1958, all from Harvard University. He was research associate in labor management history at Harvard from 1959 to 1961. From 1961 to 1965 he served as assistant professor of history at Columbia University and in 1965 became associate professor at Ohio State University. He is the author of *Steelworkers in America, The Butcher Workmen: A Study of Unionization,* and *Labor in Crisis.*

William E. Leuchtenburg, professor of history at Columbia University, was born on September 28, 1922. He received his B.A. from Cornell University in 1943 and his M.A. from Columbia University in 1944. In 1951 Columbia awarded him the Ph.D. He taught at Smith College from 1949 to 1951, was an assistant professor of history at Harvard from 1951 to 1952, and joined the faculty at Columbia in 1952. In 1959 he was made professor of history. In 1956 he lectured at the American Studies Seminar, Salzburg, Austria. He is the author of *Flood Control Politics, The Perils of Prosperity,* and *Franklin D. Roosevelt and the New Deal.*

Alfred D. Chandler, Jr., professor of history and editor of the Eisenhower Papers at The Johns Hopkins University, was born on September 15, 1918. He received both his A.B. (1940) and his M.A. (1947) from Harvard University. In 1951 he earned an M.A. from the University of North Carolina; in 1952 Harvard granted him the Ph.D. He was a research associate in history at the Massachusetts Institute of Technology in 1950; in 1951 he joined the M.I.T. faculty, and became professor in 1962. In 1963 he came to The Johns Hopkins University. He has served as a fellow in entrepreneurial history at Harvard (1952) and as academic consultant to the Naval War College (1954). In 1958–1959 he was a Guggenheim Fellow. He was the assistant editor of the *Letters of Theodore Roosevelt,* editor of

The Railroads and *Giant Enterprise,* and is the author of *Henry Varnum Poor, Business Editor* and of the Newcomen Award winner, *Strategy and Structure.*

Theodore Ropp, professor of history at Duke University, was born on May 22, 1911. His A.B. is from Oberlin College (1934), his M.A. (1936) and Ph.D. (1937) from Harvard University. He was an instructor in history at Harvard from 1937 to 1938, and was a visiting lecturer there in 1947–1948. He joined the faculty at Duke in 1938, and has held the rank of professor since 1959. He has done special research on compulsory military service and military conscription for the British Commonwealth, served as a member of the Historical Advisory Commission to the Secretary of the Army, and is director of the Policy Advisory Committee of the Historical Evaluation and Research Organization and a trustee of the American Military Institute. In 1958–1959 he was a Social Science Research Council Fellow, and in 1962–1963 was the Ernest J. King Professor of History at the Naval War College. He is the co-author of *Historical Background of the World Today,* a contributor to *Makers of Modern Strategy,* and author of *War in the Modern World.*

CONTENTS

Institutions in Modern America

INTRODUCTION

The Response to Growth: America in the Twentieth Century

by Stephen E. Ambrose

These essays, first read in the spring of 1966 as the James Schouler Lectures at The Johns Hopkins University, under the sponsorship of the Center for the Study of Recent American History, represent an attempt to analyze the way in which the United States responded to the fantastic growth rates in all fields that occurred in the first sixty-five years of the present century. Three of the lecturers concentrated on institutional innovation, the fourth on the patterns of electoral behavior and its relation to public policy. The common theme that runs through the essays is the pragmatic nature of the response, whether it be in the organization of the armed forces, the creation of the corporate structure, the problems of organized labor, or the manner of appealing to large new groups of voters. There were few philosophical underpinnings supporting the creation of the U.S. Steel Corporation, the U.S. Joint Chiefs of Staff or the Defense Department, or the C.I.O. These organizations were practical responses to practical problems. In the same way the process of politics was determined more by day-to-day needs than by ideological thought. Professors Chandler, Ropp, and Brody found structure to be of crucial importance in an analysis of the corporation, the military, and the labor union; Professor Leuchtenburg found process to be of more importance than structure in his analysis of politics. But all agree that great changes have come, and that they have come in the form of a pragmatic response to daily needs.

Co-operative activity is the core of man's experience on earth. The way in which men organize their joint activities and the institutions they build determine in large part the efficiency and the nature of society. The process by which men create and run a giant corporation which produces and distributes billions of dollars worth of goods in national and international markets, set up a huge labor union that can speak with one voice for thousands of individuals, transform an armed mob into a mass army, and through political parties make an appeal to the nation represents modern man's greatest challenge and greatest triumph. Anyone who would understand the human condition in the modern world must understand the growth, development, and effect of human institutions.

This is most obviously true in twentieth-century America, the most highly organized nation in history. The sophisticated American style of life has grown out of and within the limits set by the structure of American institutions. These institutions dominate American life, help set its tone, determine its wants and achievements, and assure its successes and failures alike. In one century the nation of rugged individualists has become the nation of giant enterprise; in the process, and in good part because of it, America has become the most productive and powerful nation in the world.

The change from a nation of small farmers, tiny factories on river banks run by a single man or family, an army of twenty-five thousand men scattered over frontier posts of a few hundred soldiers each, and political parties with almost no national organization to modern America has come about primarily because of the increase in the volume and complexity of activity. The sheer growth of the corporation, labor union, political party, and army and navy have made it imperative that those in positions of power create organizations that can efficiently manage the activity.[1]

[1] "Organization" will here be used to describe a specific corporation, political party, armed force, or labor union. "Institution" will be taken to designate the broader pattern. Thus the corporate system, or the armed forces, or political parties will be discussed as institutions, while the U.S. Steel Corporation, the U.S. Army, the Republican Party, or the United Mine Workers will be discussed as organizations.

The most salient feature of twentieth-century America has been its economic growth and the effect that growth has had on the way of life of the great bulk of the American people. The industrial transformation brought an enormous number of people into the cities, where they worked in specialized jobs that had little or no connection with the older, more self-sufficient, agrarian life. A majority of Americans, in earning their daily bread, come to deal only with other men, in sales, distribution, or service. Only a minority directly confronted seed and soil, wood and metal, pen and paper to build something new and usable from it.

This transformation in life style solved some problems while creating others. But before the nation could concentrate on the social and psychological problems inherent in an urban, industrial society, it first had to create institutions to cope with the growth itself. Even beyond that, there could have been no growth—at least on such a large scale—without intelligent institutional innovation. The natural and human resources of America made the growth possible, to be sure, but it was the ability to build institutions that were able to manage the productive process from raw material to distribution of finished product that brought it about. George E. Mowry is probably right in declaring that the two major characteristics of the urban nation from 1920 to 1960 were the rise of a mass production-mass consumption economy and the evolution of urban America. But these results only came about because Americans solved what Walter Lippmann called their greatest problem—"the management of plenty."

The "management of plenty" was the central problem in the great political debates of the century as the political parties were increasingly confronted with the problem of appealing to the new voters who lived in the new institutional framework. This confrontation began with the Progressives, continued with the New Freedom-New Nationalism campaign, was echoed in the New Deal, and appeared again in the forties and fifties. Essentially, the question was one of how to maintain growth and enjoy the fruits of production without destroying the values of democracy, for growth was creating a situation in which a very few men had a great deal of power. The cost of making sophisticated American products, with the huge expenses of research, retooling, and distribution on a mass scale, were beyond the smaller firms. Organized labor soon began to grow along with the corporations. The inescapable challenge of totalitarian ideologies and societies led to an increase of the armed forces even more spectacular than that of the civilian sector. American productive capacity and activity had become so gigantic that only huge organizations could do the managing. Those who headed the corporations, unions, and armed forces had tremendous power and posed a potential threat to the democratic system.

Yet no one could find a way to stop the concentration. In 1962 the one-time radical economist Stuart Chase was forced to agree with Roger Blough of U.S. Steel that even more concentration was needed if technological growth was to continue.

Americans wanted to have it both ways—they wanted to retain and even encourage concentration and thus enjoy its benefits while continuing to hold to their democratic values. Throughout the century the temptation to get more of the former at the expense of the latter was always great. The ideologies were there, waiting to be picked up. So were the concrete examples. Americans could look overseas and see, both on the political right and left, nations that had bought efficiency and growth at the expense of democracy. The appeal of the temptation was best seen during the great crisis of the early thirties. The "technocrats," who wanted to come to grips with modern production by junking capitalism and democracy and installing an engineer as dictator, enjoyed a great vogue even though it was short-lived.

The technocrats had a simple solution to the major problem of the twentieth century. So did the communists and the fascists. But Americans avoided, or at least could not agree to, a simple way out. Complex accommodations were required to fit the new types of organizations, value systems, and personal roles and functions demanded by the new urban, industrial, technologically committed society into a traditional democratic framework. These accommodations led to severe stresses. Nevertheless, a majority of the American people proved willing to work within the system rather than to destroy it. Even while modifying and in many ways transforming the system, they gave their support to economic, political, and military institutions that could effectively manage the new economy, polity, and society without destroying the old values.

The retention of democracy within a society of gigantic organizations is the real American success story. How it was done is a primary concern of these essays. The solutions, the essays indicate, have been mostly original. It is true, as Professor Ropp points out, that American military thought and policy before 1945 was essentially derivative, and that since World War II the armed forces have often fumbled and stumbled, meanwhile engaging in some horrendous public disputes. But if the generals and the admirals have not answered all the problems posed by the post-atomic bomb military revolution, they have at least been able to organize the vastly expanded armed forces in a fairly efficient way without destroying the traditional civil-military relationship.

In the economy, where the growth began earlier and has been steadier, the solution to the problems has been unique. Historically, the pressure for a more equitable and socially desirable allocation of the output of the economy and its resources, which began with the French Revolution, has increased with the coming of industrialization. Americans have met the demand for more efficient production through the creation of the large integrated firm, controlling its own distributing network and often producing or extracting its own raw materials. This centralization of power has been balanced partly by the growth of the modern labor union and partly by the increasing role of the government through its tax and spending policies. As Professors Chandler and Brody conclude, Americans do not yet live in the best of all possible worlds; nevertheless it is obvious that American production and the distribution of the fruits of the economy, all within a democratic framework, are the envy of the rest of the world.

Production has reached levels that are scarcely believable. In World War II the United States produced 45 per cent of the world's armament. Some two thirds of all the ships afloat in the world in 1945 were American-made. In 1955, with 6 per cent of the world's population, the United States was producing almost 50 per cent of the world's goods.

The base for this industrial capacity was laid in the nineteenth century, but it has been most impressive and momentous in the twentieth century. In 1909 the largest industrial corporation was U.S. Steel, with assets of $1,804,-000,000. In 1948 Standard Oil (New Jersey) had supplanted U.S. Steel as the largest industrial, with assets of $3,526,-000,000. In 1963 Standard Oil (New Jersey) had assets of almost $12 billion. The largest industrial had increased in size slightly less than seven times during the five decades. But that is only the beginning of the story. The third largest industrial in 1909, American Tobacco, had assets of $286 million; the third largest in 1963, Ford, had assets of nearly $6 billion, a more than twenty-fold increase. The hundredth largest industrial in 1909, American Steel Foundries, had $25 million in assets; the hundredth largest in 1963, Reynolds, had assets of $1,028,059,000, almost a forty-fold increase. The smaller firms were catching up with the larger ones, and they all had to face and overcome the problems of organization and management once reserved for the giants.

Growth was just as great in other fields. In 1900 organized labor had a total membership of 868,000; in 1962 labor had over 18 million. This huge increase brought crucial management problems not only to the federations at the top but also to each of the individual national unions. The U.S. Army, which barely reached the one million mark in manpower during the Civil War, rose to just under 2.5 million during World War I. In 1945, before demobilization began, it numbered 8,291,336, and total military personnel rose to over 12 million. In 1865 the War Department spent $1,031,323,361. In 1918 the figure was $5.5 billion. In the single year of 1945 the Department spent just under $50 billion. In January, 1942, a colonel on the Munitions Board whose specialty was machine tools was given $19 million and told to spend it before June.

Activity on these levels required, indeed dictated, organizational change. In the last decade of the nineteenth and first decade of the twentieth century most large firms, labor unions, and the armed forces took on their modern form, but continued and increased growth forced further structural modifications, and those who refused to change stagnated. The E. I. du Pont de Nemours company, for example, after transforming itself from a family firm into a modern corporation in 1903, had to reorganize again after World War I. The U.S. Army, which underwent only two significant organizational changes in the nineteenth century, has had six in the twentieth century. The failure of the American Federation of Labor to reorganize to meet new needs and demands brought on labor's civil war. Perhaps the inability or refusal of the great political parties to modify their organizations to meet the needs of an urban industrial society has been one factor in bringing about the politics of statics which Professor Leuchtenburg analyzes. As Professor Chandler has pointed out (in *Strategy and Structure*), "growth without structural adjustment can only lead to . . . inefficiency."

While the United States has grown enormously in the past two generations and while a crucial factor in this growth has been institutional innovation, institutional history has received little systematic study. All concede its importance, but few work in the area. The reasons are simple enough. Institutional history can never be as dramatic as biography or as exciting as the treatment of an event. The development of institutions is a continuing process, and it is difficult to choose a single happening and center the narrative around it. The crucial decision-making process as it affects human beings seems absent in institutional history because the decisions involved in reshaping the structure of an organization are a step removed from the decisions which affect human lives. The decisions taken by an organization which do have a direct effect seem faceless and machine-made and thus, although important, colorless.

A further problem is that those who begin working on institutional history are tempted to abandon the problem of how the structure came about and how it works, and to concentrate on the decisions. The historian who begins working on the Combined Chiefs of Staff in World War II, for example, might quickly move away from an analysis of the organization into a discussion of why the Chiefs decided to make the Mediterranean the main theater of war in 1943. This is an important and surely a fascinating question, but it is usually broken down by asking what the President thought, what the Prime Minister thought, and what each individual member of the Chiefs of Staff thought. The organization fades into the background.

Yet the structure of the organization determined in large part what the decision would be, for the individual Chiefs were dependent on their sources of information. If the organization were effective, the various Chiefs would see all the relevant information and have numerous alternatives from which to choose. If it were ineffective, they would see only parts of the situation and would be forced into a single line of action dictated by the incomplete information.

Even information is only a part of the problem, for the organization can set additional limits on the freedom of action of those at the top. In the sixties Secretary of Defense Robert McNamara's problem has not been so much an absence of information as it has been an ingrained hostility to change. He has had little difficulty in working out both his reorganization plans and his ideas for a new defense policy, but he has encountered enormous difficulty in attempting to persuade career officials in the department to co-operate. President John Kennedy had to face the same situation in his dealings with the State Department. So do those who would change either General Motors' structure or the basic styling of its automobiles. It was resistance to change that led to the A.F. of L.'s great failure in the thirties.

An examination of the internal workings of American institutions is the starting point for an understanding of twentieth-century America. The topic is intrinsically interesting, indeed fascinating. But, because few historians have chosen to accept the challenge, the historical profession as a whole has come dangerously close to abandoning the field to the social scientists. The standard work on the A.F. of L. in the time of Gompers is by an economist. The best studies of the organization of the armed forces are by sociologists and political scientists. Political scientists also have a virtual monopoly on the problems of the workings of the government and party organization. Yet surely in these fields the historian, with his traditional suspicion of theory and method and his respect for the data, can make significant contributions.

Fortunately, the interest of American historians in the institution and the history of organizations is growing. Following a recent intensive investigation of the American historical profession today, John Higham concluded that the most exciting work going on was in the application of psychological concepts to history and in the work of the institutional historians:

> American historians have not yielded wholly to the psychologizing trend. Among those who still respect the force of overt principles, a strain of rationalism persists. It is also reappearing among a small but rising number of historians who are taking a fresh look at organization patterns. The latter wish to know how groups and agencies—such as political parties, corporations, and communities—have molded behavior and regulated the distribution of power. Derived partly from studies in entrepreneurial and business history and partly from contemporary American sociology, this kind of history is less concerned with motives than with structure and process. It shows men managing and being managed through rational systems of control and communication. Perhaps we may call this the new institutionalism. . . . Although the institutionalists thus far have not gone much beyond the monographic level, the breadth and import of their contributions seem sure to grow.

The authors of these essays hope that they will encourage even more American historians to venture into the important fields of institutional history and the process of politics.

I

THE EXPANSION OF THE AMERICAN LABOR MOVEMENT: INSTITUTIONAL SOURCES OF STIMULUS AND RESTRAINT

by David Brody

On December 29, 1932, George E. Barnett, dean of Johns Hopkins labor economists, delivered the presidential address before the American Economic Association. His speech had an ironic ring, for, at the close of a distinguished career, Professor Barnett was consigning the subject of his scholarship to a place of secondary interest. Trade unionism, he said, was exercising "lessening importance . . . in American economic organization." Membership stood below three million, a mark passed fifteen years before. Professor Barnett traced labor's decline back beyond the great depression which was raging at the time of his address. Basic weaknesses had emerged during the previous decade, when for the first time the union movement had failed to capitalize on prosperity. Professor Barnett drew a dark conclusion: "I see no reason to believe that American trade unionism will so revolutionize itself within a short period as to become in the next decade a more potent social influence than it has been in the past decade."[1]

Yet inside of six months organized labor was resurgent. It recovered the losses of a decade in two years, gained another three million workmen between 1935 and 1938, and reached fourteen million members in a final surge during

[1] George E. Barnett, "American Trade Unionism and Social Insurance," *American Economic Review,* XXIII (March, 1933), 1, 6. Barnett did offer one hope for the labor movement. The A.F. of L. had just reversed a long-standing position and had come out for public unemployment insurance. Barnett suggested that the union movement might continue to play an important role as an instigator of government action.

the war years. "Measured in numbers, political influence, economic weight, or by any other yardstick," the president of the United States Chamber of Commerce acknowledged in 1944, "labor is a power in our land."[2] It was a far cry from the future predicted by Professor Barnett in 1932.

His miscalculation suggests a way of looking at the growth of the modern labor movement. American trade unionism housed contradictory tendencies toward the unorganized—a propensity toward rigid restriction and an opposing responsive capacity for growth. The expansive tendency, rarely very marked since the early years, had fallen entirely from sight during the twenties and early thirties. Nor would a close study of trade unions have predicted the resurgence of the expansive phase. For the trigger was not in the labor movement, but in the larger environment. Professor Barnett's pessimism in 1932 was well founded (and almost uniformly shared): he could not foresee the impending turn of national events, nor, even had he done so, would the recent past have suggested the trade unions' capacity to respond to the opportunity granted by the great depression and the New Deal.

This dualism had its roots in the formative period of American unionism in the late nineteenth century. The movement shaped itself on a modest appraisal of its situation in American society. Nineteenth-century reformers had envisaged all "producers"—that is, nearly everyone—marching toward a co-operative commonwealth. Only saloonkeepers, lawyers, and stockbrokers had been excluded from the Knights of Labor. The optimism of labor reformers rested on their denial of class conflict. Trade unionists saw a harsher reality—a nation permanently divided into contending classes by the Industrial Revolution. They claimed only one group for the union movement, the wage workers, and rigidly excluded everyone else. But, if American labor was class-conscious, it was so in a peculiarly American way. In

[2] Eric Johnston, *America Unlimited* (New York, 1944), p. 176.

this pluralistic society, men thought of themselves not only as workers, but as Catholics, Republicans, Odd Fellows, and much else besides. Trade unionism could not contradict those other loyalties. Nor could it pursue goals other than those of concern to its members.[3] And American workingmen were, in Selig Perlman's phrase, "job-conscious." They confined their interests, as workers, to the terms of their employment. Voluntary associations that they were, trade unions could lead only where the rank and file would follow—a narrow channel indeed.

No one saw more steadily nor better articulated the consequences of these modest circumstances than did Samuel Gompers. Not that he repudiated his youthful dreams ("I believe with the most advanced thinkers as to ultimate ends including the abolition of the wage system," he was still saying in 1887), but he set them aside and, eventually, left them behind. They were beyond the means and will of American labor. Gompers turned to the immediate and the possible. The labor movement, he explained, attempted "to work along the lines of least resistance; to accomplish the best results in improving the condition of the working people . . . each day making it a better day than the one that had gone before. . . . And wherever that may lead . . . so far in my time and my age I decline . . . to be labelled by any particular ism." The trade unionist concerned himself only with the pursuit of "more, more, more, now."[4]

The movement likewise tailored its methods to its limitations. Economic action, not politics, seemed labor's best hope. Given a constituency limited in numbers and in commitment, the union movement could not be very strong in the political arena. Moreover, the state—the one coercive agency in American society—posed the greatest potential

[3] For the influence of the Catholic church on the A.F. of L., for example, see Marc Karson, *American Labor Unions and Politics, 1900–1918* (Carbondale, Ill., 1958), ch. IX.

[4] Philip S. Foner, *History of the Labor Movement in the United States* (3 vols.; New York, 1947–), II, p. 177; United States Commission on Industrial Relations, *Final Report and Testimony* (11 vols.; Washington, D.C., 1916), II, p. 1528; Louis D. Reed, *The Labor Philosophy of Samuel Gompers* (New York, 1930), pp. 18 ff.

danger to labor. As voluntary associations, finally, trade unions found little organizational benefit in legislative gains. Compulsory unemployment insurance, William Green once warned, would "pull at our vitals and destroy our trade union structure." Collective bargaining, on the other hand, gave unions a continuing function and a claim on the members. Nineteenth-century conditions encouraged the economic bias; industrial expansion and labor shortages had consistently favored the bargaining position of American working men. Gompers elevated these considerations into ruling principles. His doctrine of "voluntarism" located the labor movement firmly in the private sector of American life. Unions should never seek "at the hands of the government what they could accomplish by their own initiative and activities." A companion doctrine, drawn from early Marxist lessons, sustained the basic tactical position of American labor: "Economic need and economic betterment could best be served by mobilizing and controlling economic power."[5]

"Pure and simple" unionism, as Gompers' formulation came to be known, really described a tendency rooted in American labor organization. The earliest local unions, Philip Taft has shown, devoted themselves to economic action, and quickly learned to resist the temptations of politics and reform. Starting with the International Typographical Union in 1852, local bodies of the same craft began to form national unions. It was further proof of the commitment to economic unionism. The transportation revolution was nationalizing American markets. To function effectively in the economic sphere, labor organization had to parallel that change. Thus initiated, the national unions gradually evolved the essential controls over membership standards, over strikes, and over collective bargaining. The prime institutions for economic action, the national unions, became the dominant units of American trade unionism. When it

[5] James O. Morris, *Conflict within the AFL* (Ithaca, N.Y., 1958), pp. 138–39; Reed, *Labor Philosophy of Gompers,* p. 118; Samuel Gompers, *Seventy Years of Life and Labor* (2 vols.; New York, 1925).

was formed in 1886, the American Federation of Labor recognized their supremacy in its basic laws.[6]

The next two decades permanently validated the trade union approach. The stubborn strain of politics and reform in American labor finally withered away with the collapse of the Knights of Labor and a series of political fiascoes. The trade unions, meanwhile, were attaining institutional stability. In the eighteen nineties they survived intact a major depression for the first time. When prosperity returned, the movement burst forward. From a base of half a million in 1897, membership more than quadrupled in five years, and collective bargaining made notable headway. An expanding future seemed to lie before a movement (as Gompers had said) "founded on eminently practical questions."

But at that point American trade unionism became the victim of a historical irony. Just as the movement crystallized on the basis of nineteenth-century conditions, its environment changed drastically. The mass production revolution occurred, sharpening management opposition to collective bargaining, increasing the means for fighting unions, and undermining the union strategy of control of the labor market. Trade unionism discovered itself barred from the heart of the American economy—the great industries characterized by mass production technology and large-scale business organization. Employer opposition quickly spread beyond these confines. In 1903 the movement came under the fire of open-shop organizations headed by the National Association of Manufacturers. Public authorities joined the attack. The courts turned their injunction powers and the Sherman Anti-Trust Act against the trade unions, blunting the force of the strike and the boycott. Gompers' fear of the state now found ample justification.

These reversals exposed an unforeseen limitation of a movement shaped by pure and simple doctrine: an incapacity to respond to adverse change. Its modest self-assessment rendered American trade unionism essentially a passive agent

[6] Philip Taft, "On the Origins of Business Unionism," *Industrial and Labor Relations Review,* XVII (October, 1963), 20–38; Lloyd Ulman, *The Rise of the National Union* (Cambridge, Mass., 1955).

in relation to its surrounding environment. Labor unions operated *in,* not *against,* the economic setting. They lacked the capacity, or even the intention, of influencing the technological change that was undermining craft union strength. The vast resources of the giant corporations posed an equal obstacle to the growth of organized labor. Yet the A.F. of L. did not lead in the antitrust movement. (Indeed, Gompers accepted business concentration as an aspect of economic evolution.) Only special circumstances and an existing bargaining relationship, such as existed in the demoralized coal and clothing industries of the nineteen twenties, spurred trade unions to a direct concern with their industrial environment.

Nor could organized labor take the more obvious path of politics to alter its environment. Legislation that might redress in a direct way the balance between labor and management—a Wagner act—was ruled out. "In the demand for collective bargaining labor has never asked that it be gained by law" was the A.F. of L. response in 1919 to a bill providing for collective bargaining in industries engaged in interstate commerce.[7] Some issues did, of course, demand political answers. When opponents employed public weapons, labor had to defend itself by political means. Likewise, trade unionists saw the benefits of public controls over the labor supply, for example, in the restriction of immigration and the regulation of child and female labor. But even on this limited scale, the union movement scored only modest success. Trade unionism was not primarily designed for political action. Authority and money accumulated in the national unions rather than in labor's political arms—the city centrals, the state federations, the A.F. of L. itself.[8] Organized labor lacked political means, even after its aggressive shift in 1906 from lobbying tactics to electioneering for its friends and against its enemies. The trade union environment had to be taken as it was in the early twentieth century.

[7] Morris, *Conflict within the AFL,* p. 38.

[8] See, for example, Irwin Yellowitz, *Labor and the Progressive Movement in New York State, 1897–1916* (Ithaca, N.Y., 1965).

That left the alternative of accommodation. A conciliatory line offered one possibility. The A.F. of L. assiduously wooed big business, first in the National Civic Federation, and then, in the nineteen twenties, in a campaign (using the model of the Baltimore and Ohio plan) for greater industrial efficiency. Neither effort had much success, as Gompers' faith in economic power should have foreseen. Not conciliation but a more intelligent response to economic reality was what offered hope for the expansion of American trade unionism. That, too, proved beyond the capacity of the labor movement in a hostile environment.

The failing was not accidental; it was firmly rooted in the foundations of American organized labor. To begin with, there was the rule of trade autonomy—that is, the sovereignty of the national unions. Beyond being a safeguard for the organizations forming the A.F. of L., trade autonomy reflected the importance of the national unions as the agencies carrying on the primary functions of the movement. They had the right, Gompers had said from the beginning, "to do as they think is just and proper in matters of their own trades, without the let or hindrance of any other body of men. . . ." The Federation, Gompers reminded the delegates in his last speech to an A.F. of L. convention, was "an organization that had no power and no authority except of a voluntary character."[9] No one outside the power structure of the national unions—and that category included some of the men best able to do the job—had the means to organize the unorganized. Unionization depended ultimately on the national unions. And they, for reasons entirely sound from their standpoint, held back on the task.

The national unions had taken shape—the transformation of the Cigarmakers' Union in the late eighteen seventies was the model instance—as vehicles for collective bargaining and the exertion of economic force. That institutional development placed restraints on the organizing function, once a stable membership was built up, internal order created, and vested interests formed. Thereafter, unionizing

[9] Reed, *Labor Philosophy of Gompers,* p. 149; Bernard Mandel, *Samuel Gompers* (Yellow Springs, Ohio, 1963), p. 524.

activities were considered essential under only one condition—when the lack of organization threatened the status quo. But such pressure did not touch some of the strongest of trade unions. The Teamsters, the construction trades, and certain other craft unions operated in local product markets. The local unions moved heaven and earth to organize their own areas, but they did not consider it vital for local markets elsewhere to be organized nor, in their own territories, workmen of their trades whose employers did not compete with the union enterprises. The primary unions in the basic industries found sheltered spots, even if these were pitifully small, in which they could survive.[10] Except for such fields as coal and clothing, no economic imperatives drove the national unions into unorganized areas.

Then why hold so stubbornly to jurisdictions there? In part, the national unions were merely exploiting their prerogative as autonomous organizations: no authority could force them to relinquish an established claim, nor make them answerable for how they exercised their territorial rights. The national unions were also motivated by more positive considerations. The unorganized jurisdictions were filled with potential dues-paying members (which hence had a property value akin to a natural resource) and in some instances had strategic importance. The United Brotherhood of Carpenters fought relentlessly to secure jurisdiction over the entire wood industry, destroying the vigorous Amalgamated Wood Workers in the process. The objective was not so much to bring in the woodworkers as to "police" the industry. The Carpenters wanted, first, to protect their jobs should technological change shift work into the mills, and, second, to control the suppliers of unionized construction markets.[11] So the national unions blocked any transfer of jurisdiction over workmen whom they lacked compelling reasons to organize.

Further calculations tipped the scales of tough-minded trade unionists against acting without an imperative reason. Finances had become of first importance to the functioning

[10] See, for example, David Brody, *Steelworkers in America* (Cambridge, Mass., 1960), ch. III.

[11] Robert A. Christie, *Empire in Wood* (Ithaca, N.Y., 1956).

of labor unions. Defense funds, intricate revenue systems, and an accounting mentality had developed. Should money be diverted from regular purposes to new areas? Would the probable advantages to the existing membership justify the expenditure? The internal structure, reflecting the local market fields in which many A.F. of L. unions operated, often left much authority and income in the hands of the local unions and district bodies. Would they support organizing activities of little direct concern to them? The unions had evolved a career leadership and a one-party political system. Might not an influx of new members, especially those not drawn from a union's normal area of operation, endanger internal stability?

The list of questions lengthened. The organizing drives in mass production industries demanded a joint effort. Would other national unions co-operate and carry a fair share of the work? (The disastrous steel drive of 1919 suggested the problems in this area.[12]) Trade unions, as voluntary associations, depended on rank and file loyalty. The unorganized were largely recent immigrants and Negroes. Might they not alienate the native-born unionists? Could mass production workers show the discipline and order essential for rational strike action and collective bargaining? (A long train of union defeats indicated how difficult it was to control freshly organized industrial workers.)

These hard questions did not all bear or bear with equal weight on every decision involving non-union ground. But responsible leaders had always to strike a balance between the narrow interests of their existing organizations and the claims of the unorganized. In an era when, in any case, the odds were weighted heavily against success, that calculation restrained the national unions as organizing agencies.

So Professor Barnett rightly despaired of American trade unionism in 1932. The movement seemed locked to the skilled occupations, and exerted power in but a handful of industries. During the twenties only the building trades flourished. Between 1920 and 1926, thirty-three unions,

[12] David Brody, *Labor in Crisis: The Steel Strike of 1919* (Philadelphia, 1965).

primarily in manufacturing, shrank in membership by nearly 60 per cent. Nor was there any sign of an inner revolution. One observer in 1926 found most labor leaders "a curious blending of defeatism with complacency." A harsher critic in 1929 dismissed the A.F. of L. as "a life raft—though now beginning to get waterlogged—for skilled labor." Three years of depression reduced the movement by another half-million members and rendered even the strongest unions ineffective in collective bargaining.[13] At the end of 1932, as Professor Barnett observed, the labor movement, seemingly, faced a dark future.

The next months abruptly transformed the trade union environment. The depression finally broke down the acquiescent relationship fostered by welfare capitalism and aroused industrial workers to action. During the early period of the N.R.A., a spontaneous push for organization developed. It was a sight, said William Green, "that even the old, tried veterans of our movement never saw before."[14] The depression also created a new political situation. Administrations came to power in Washington and in key states which, both from conviction and expediency, championed the cause of labor. Among the benefits to the unions, none held greater importance than the legislation that granted new rights and privileges to labor. The rank and file upheaval and political changes, together with the economic impact of the depression, cut down the defenses of capital. Even the mightiest of corporations became vulnerable to unionization during the thirties.

The labor movement was the beneficiary, not the agent, of the sudden turn in its fortunes. Only in politics did trade unions contribute—and even there but modestly—to the alteration of the environment. But this activated within the movement powerful pressures for expansion. To have at-

[13] David Saposs, *Left Wing Unionism* (New York, 1926), pp. 115–16; Irving Bernstein, *The Lean Years* (Boston, 1960), pp. 84, 335; Sumner Slichter, "The Current Labor Policies of American Industries," *Quarterly Journal of Economics,* XLIII (May, 1929), 427.

[14] American Federation of Labor, *Proceedings* (1933), p. 8.

tempted to unionize the basic industries earlier, John L. Lewis admitted in 1935, "would have been suicide for organized labor and would have resulted in complete failure. But now, the time is ripe; and now the time to do these things is here. Let us do them."[15]

That decision, it is essential to see, sprang from the logic of trade unionism no less than had the opposite conclusion of earlier years. John L. Lewis was drawn directly from the pure and simple tradition of the American labor movement. He represented, one writer noted in 1925, "the older type of labor executive, autocratic, more aggressive than penetrating, unreceptive to the new principle[s], a protagonist of simple unionism." Conservative in politics, dictatorial as president of the United Mine Workers, conventional in collective bargaining despite the collapse of the coal trade, Lewis seemed in the twenties, as one observer wrote, "the grand walking delegate, the glorified organizer, the perfect boss in American labor."[16] Yet John L. Lewis was the man who instantly sprang to the head of the group pressing for action after the start of the New Deal. "It's middling tough for one who fought John L. so long and bitterly to pay this tribute," confessed a labor journalist in 1933, "but give the devil his dues. John turned out to be the only archangel among the angels with fallen arches of the A.F. of L. crowd."[17] Ambition and personal drive assuredly contributed to Lewis' apparent transformation—he was, as Francis Biddle later said, very nearly a great man—but his efforts were wholly explicable in trade union terms. That statement holds also for Sidney Hillman, David Dubinsky, Charles Howard, and the lesser men who gathered around Lewis. Observing them at the end of 1933, David Saposs found "no ideological difference distinguishing them from the old guard. . . . They differ from the old guard on the best way to take advan-

[15] Saul Alinsky, *John L. Lewis* (New York, 1949), p. 80. On union influence on labor legislation, see Irving Bernstein, *New Deal Collective Bargaining Policy* (Berkeley, Calif., 1950).

[16] Cecil Carnes, *John L. Lewis* (New York, 1936), pp. 139, 145.

[17] Oscar Ameringer, clipping, n.d. [1933], John Brophy Papers, Catholic University of America.

tage of the opportunity presented by government intervention. . . ."[18]

The industrial union group was responding, first of all, to the historical sense of obligation to the unorganized. Gompers had always insisted that the A.F. of L. spoke for all wage earners, not just union men, and he had never ceased working for the spread of labor organization. Even when it grew remote from the concerns of many craft union leaders, they never could deny the goal of organizing the unorganized. The low point came in the twenties, when prosperity and welfare capitalism began to undermine confidence in the social value of labor organization. The depression revived labor's sense of indignation. In 1932, the A.F. of L. came out for public unemployment insurance, a startling departure from the rule of voluntarism. The mild William Green astonished the entire country when he threatened "forceful methods" to shorten hours and increase wages. "We have simply come to what we are determined shall be the end of the road of suffering." That sentiment grew especially compelling among the advocates of industrial unionism. "The labor movement is organized upon a principle that the strong shall help the weak," John L. Lewis pleaded before the A.F. of L. convention of 1935. "Isn't it right that we should contribute something of our own strength . . . toward those less fortunately situated. . . . Organize the unorganized and in so doing you make the American Federation of Labor the greatest instrumentality that has ever been forged in the history of modern civilization to befriend the cause of humanity and champion human rights."[19]

But trade unionists had always held realism in higher regard than compassion. The American setting denied them the luxury of sacrificing power for ideals. The industrial unionists shared that tough-minded assumption. "A union should be regarded as . . . progressive when it brings about a new condition in industry through the exercise of its

[18] David Saposs, "The New Labor Progressives," *New Republic* (January 24, 1934), pp. 300–2.

[19] Chester M. Wright, "Labor Unfurls Its Battle Flags," *Nation's Business,* XXXI (February, 1933), 13–15; A.F. of L., *Proceedings* (1935), pp. 541–42.

power," Sidney Hillman had argued in 1928. "Policy and strategy are only the means to the end, and the end is the realization of power for the movement."[20] Union men of vision had always insisted that greater organization would strengthen all the unions in the movement, and now so did the industrial unionists. But equally important was the narrower calculation habitual to the national unions. The United Mine Workers had just survived a harrowing decade, in which its troubles had derived largely from the competition of non-union coal fields. Now, rescued by the National Industrial Recovery Act, Lewis was determined to secure his union from that threat, and his objective required the unionization of the steel industry. John Brophy, Lewis' lieutenant, emphasized the connection in his memoirs: "Steel was the key to understanding Lewis' policy; the mine workers would never be safe until steel was unionized. . . . Lewis and the UMW, intent on steel, were driven to create the CIO, because there was no other way to get the job in steel done."[21] The Clothing Workers and the Ladies' Garment Workers were similarly situated. Both waged a constant battle against non-union competition, and hence saw specific benefits in the organization of related industries. So the narrow considerations of pure and simple unionism weighed heavily in the thinking of the industrial unionists.

Political change added another element to their calculations. Trade unionists had always concentrated on economic power, and, whether A.F. of L. or C.I.O., they continued to do so in the thirties. But politics was now looming larger. For one thing, much was at stake. The depression had drawn the government decisively into labor's sphere. On the other hand, political patterns had altered. The New Deal was responsive to organized labor, provided only that its voice was strong. The automobile code had worked out badly, Lewis observed, because labor weakness (in this case, the lack of a national union) permitted "the Recovery Ad-

[20] Sidney Hillman, "Labor Attitudes," in *American Labor Dynamics*, ed. J. B. S. Hardman (New York, 1928), pp. 292–93.

[21] John Brophy, *A Miner's Life*, ed. John O. P. Hall (Madison, Wis., 1964), p. 249; David Saposs, "Industrial Unionism," *Journal of Political Economy*, XLIII (February, 1935), 81; A.F. of L., *Proceedings* (1935), p. 539.

ministration and the White House to make decisions without fear of any successful challenge from the American Federation of Labor."[22] The industrial unionists were particularly sensitive to political factors partly because of their experience in Washington during the N.R.A. period, partly from the special need for government regulation in their industries, and in some cases from past conviction. A large-scale labor movement seemed to them essential to meet the political demands of the Roosevelt era.

Not all trade unionists responded to these calculations. Older restraints operated in key craft organizations and, indeed, grew more deeply entrenched in the face of challenge. Between 1933 and 1935 their contribution, either in the way of money or co-operation, fell short of past attempts to organize the basic industries, and they embraced more stubbornly the principles of trade autonomy and exclusive jurisdiction. The craft unions would not countenance the by-passing of ineffectual unions with major jurisdictions, nor would they themselves forego their claims to men in the mass production fields. "We are not going to desert the fundamental principles on which [the craft unions] have lived and are living to help you organize men who have never been organized," Daniel Tobin of the Teamsters bluntly told John L. Lewis at a climactic meeting in May, 1935. That obstinacy only revealed the intensity of the expansionist impulse activated by the changed environment. "We were all convinced," John Brophy recalled of a strategy meeting held soon after, "that in the temper of the times, there was a great opportunity to push forward . . . that if the delay was continued too long, it would mean the opportunity would run out on us, and we would lose a chance that only comes once in a long while."[23] To exploit it, the industrial unionists finally resorted to independent action.

Violating though it did labor's cardinal rule against dual unionism, that undertaking was entirely logical from a trade

[22] Philip Taft, *The A.F. of L. from the Death of Gompers to the Merger* (New York, 1959), p. 104.

[23] American Federation of Labor Executive Council, Minutes, April 30–May 7, 1935, p. 124; John Brophy Memoir, Oral History Collection, Columbia University, p. 553.

union standpoint. Lewis insisted that his were "not the objectives of someone else, but the declared objectives of the American Federation of Labor. . . ." Only one question concerned him: what would work? For mass production workers, Lewis answered, only industrial unions. The issue of structure no longer held ideological significance, as it earlier had among radicals bent on transforming the labor movement. In the thirties the matter became a practical one. Industrial workers—"mass-minded," as William Green described them—resisted division into separate unions. Nor had this arrangement in the past provided the degree of unity that seemed essential in confronting the giant corporations. So rubber, steel, and auto unions had to be formed on an industrial basis. Entirely pragmatic in his view of the structural issue, Lewis in late 1934 tried to make a bargain that would preserve the essentials: let industrial jurisdictions be granted on a temporary basis; the craft unions that so desired could exercise their claims later, when division would not endanger the mass production unions.[24]

From that point on, considerations of power—as characteristic as Lewis' pragmatism in the labor movement—dominated and forced the dispute over structure to the point of an open split. The craft unions, after seeming to agree, quickly backed away from Lewis' proposition. Could they exercise their jurisdictions after unionization had occurred on an industrial basis? Not if the new unions were strong enough to prevent it. For all the attention to legality, in the end power counted in the labor movement. So the craft unions excluded specific groups from the jurisdictions of the Auto Workers and the Rubber Workers at meetings of the A.F. of L. Executive Council in early 1935. They had enough votes later in the year to ratify that action at the fateful A.F. of L. convention in Atlantic City. But a ballot could not settle this issue. The Lewis group had a vital interest and the means to pursue it. In the past, the labor movement had always given in to that combination—hence, among other things, the granting of industrial jurisdiction to the Mine

[24] For an elaboration of this view, see my essay, "The Emergence of Mass-Production Unionism," in *Change and Continuity in Twentieth Century America,* ed. John Braeman *et al.* (Columbus, Ohio, 1964).

Workers in 1901. Now in the thirties a unique situation faced the A.F. of L.: a confrontation of two power blocs with vital interests. Given the fact that Lewis considered it essential to organize mass production workers, his decision to ignore the A.F. of L. resolution against industrial unionism was sound from a trade union standpoint. Nor, curiously, was it out of character for craft chieftains such as William Hutcheson—himself a master of *machtpolitik*—to raise their hands in horror over Lewis' violation of majority rule and exclusive jurisdiction. In a labor movement lacking a strong central authority, legality and power politics existed side by side. The only surprising feature was that, without much regard for the constitutional niceties, the craft unions should have carried their disapproval to the extreme of reading the industrial union group out of the American Federation of Labor and so transformed the Committee for Industrial Organization into a rival federation.

Free as it was to experiment, the C.I.O. actually drew heavily on the strengths and practices of American trade unionism. The organizing drives, of course, posed special, and to some degree new, problems. The mass production workers were aroused; their Negro and immigrant elements injected further resentments and sensitivities; and the Wagner act gave them a free choice of union representation. In this situation, fresh tactics necessarily emerged, and the C.I.O. had special advantages in the struggle to win rank and file support. Yet the C.I.O. was not departing from basic trade union patterns. With the exception of the major innovation of the "organizing committee" (such as the Steel Workers Organizing Committee), the structural arrangements followed those already in existence, and much of the C.I.O. effectiveness depended on traditional characteristics. American labor unions emphasized financial strength, so the C.I.O. could throw funds into organizing work on a massive scale; they employed a staff of professionals, so a cadre of organizers was immediately available; they had autocratic leadership, so the allocation of their resources raised no effective opposition. "We're in a position to throw our weight about," John L. Lewis told his subordinates after the United Mine Workers had re-established itself in the coal industry. "We have some resources. We have some money and some manpower to put into a struggle of this kind."[25]

A final ingredient of C.I.O. success derived from the established movement—namely, an ability to exploit the American left wing. The C.I.O. attracted able leaders who, from a variety of standpoints, rejected the standing order. Some of Lewis' former enemies, such as John Brophy, Adolph Germer, and Powers Hapgood, swallowed their bitterness and followed Lewis now because he seemed the key to social change. Germer, who had been secretary of the Socialist Party, quit because, as he explained, it was a time for action, not talk. Another socialist, who also had begun to concentrate on union affairs, agreed "that working in an economic organization we are likely to accomplish more now than working in the party, as it is now constituted."[26] The moderate American left had always been drawn to the trade union movement when it gave promise of effectiveness—as it did in the thirties. The other side of the coin was that left-wingers were welcomed into the C.I.O. That, too, was in keeping with the trade union past. As a voluntary association in a pluralistic society, the labor movement necessarily judged men by performance, not by belief or by other affiliations. Participants had only to adhere to the code of priorities: while in the role of trade unionists, they had to place union objectives first. Socialists had functioned in the labor movement on this basis for many years. John L. Lewis was willing to accept even Communists, not only because (as he said) he felt confident that he could control them, but because the labor movement could control them: their participation depended on devotion to trade union,

[25] John Brophy Memoir, Oral History Collection, Columbia University, p. 555.

[26] Marx Lewis to Adolph Germer, March 31, 1934, Germer Papers, University of Wisconsin. There had also been a radical left wing which had always insisted on dual unionism, i.e., no participation in the conservative movement. By the thirties, the radical left had been supplanted, except for fragments, by the Communist Party; and its relations with organized labor were determined, not by the historical positions of the American left, but by instructions from Moscow. As it happened, the Party reverted to a policy of boring from within in 1935, and its members became available to the C.I.O.

that is, collective bargaining, objectives. The cold war subsequently created international issues of greater moment to labor, and resulted in the expulsion of Communist-dominated unions from the C.I.O. in 1949.[27] But during the organizing period, for reasons fixed in the trade union past, the C.I.O. received a mighty contribution from left-wingers for its non-radical purposes.

After the great victories against General Motors and United States Steel in early 1937, quick progress to complete unionization was anticipated. The road, however, proved unexpectedly difficult. New Deal legislation and depression conditions permitted organizations to gain a foothold, but not to secure themselves, in the basic industries. Only further environmental changes—the return of prosperity after 1939 and then the emergency conditions of World War II—made collective bargaining effective and completed the unionizing process. By 1946, the C.I.O. had come close to its goal in the mass production sector of the economy.

That achievement, fundamental as it was, did not exhaust labor's capacity to expand in a favorable environment. Another pattern of growth, more conventional initially but perhaps of larger significance in the long run, accompanied the triumph of industrial organization. The A.F. of L. was itself expanding. It increased just as rapidly as did the C.I.O. for the first decade after the split, and then in the later forties began to outdistance its smaller rival. By the

[27] An essential distinction must be drawn here between attitudes toward Communists based on internal politics and on fundamental ideological differences. The Communists were fought within C.I.O. unions on the former grounds (in fact, Lewis had long since barred them from the United Mine Workers) because the Communists operated as disciplined factions in the struggle for internal control. The issue was over power, not over basic policies. When the Communists won out, they did not reorient their organizations away from trade union objectives—hence the successful union careers of men like Harry Bridges, Julius Emspak, and Ben Gold. And where they did, as in the United Automobile Workers and the National Maritime Union in the mid-forties, the Communists quickly lost their hold. On the last point, see B. J. Widick and Irving Howe, *The UAW and Walter Reuther* (New York, 1949), chs. V, VII; David Saposs, *Communism in American Unions* (New York, 1959), pp. 192–93.

time of the merger in 1955, the A.F. of L. represented over ten million men, the C.I.O. five million.

Mass production industry had made a peculiarly difficult demand of the labor movement—namely, that established national unions subordinate their own institutional interests and encourage an organizational growth that would not accrue to them. Only the men initiating the C.I.O. had been able to jump that gap—to think, as Sidney Hillman said, "in terms of the whole labor movement."[28] The others continued to concentrate first of all on their own national unions, as the structure and logic of American trade unionism had always dictated. But that narrower focus did not render the A.F. of L. unions ineffectual; on the contrary, after 1935 it stimulated expansion on a vast scale within the existing framework of the national unions. Between 1936 and 1941, the Machinists grew from 105,000 to 284,000, the building trades unions from 650,000 to 893,000. The Teamsters, never larger than 100,000 before 1933, reached 170,000 in 1936, 530,000 in 1941, and 1,300,000 in 1955. Of the six biggest national unions in the early sixties, four had been old-line A.F. of L. unions—Teamsters, Machinists, Electrical Workers, Carpenters.[29]

Initially, these craft unions had seen no more than an opportunity to fill in their basic occupational jurisdictions. They had opposed the industrial union group so stubbornly because at last the craft workers in mass production industries had seemed accessible to them. But then a quiet revolution occurred: A.F. of L. unions began to expand beyond their favored job groups. The exclusive view continued to prevail in some quarters. "No organizing campaign was put into effect by our International office to recruit membership in wholesale lots," the Bricklayers' officers assured the membership in 1938. "We insisted that our unions function for the benefit of those who had remained loyal to the organization through times of stress. . . ."[30] But new conditions increasingly overwhelmed that old-line viewpoint.

[28] Matthew Josephson, *Sidney Hillman* (New York, 1952), p. 382.

[29] *Monthly Labor Review* (May, 1964), p. 506.

[30] Walter Galenson, *The CIO Challenge to the AFL* (Cambridge, Mass., 1960), p. 521.

The calculations remained characteristically trade union, but the conclusion now pointed in the direction of expansion—toward bringing in lower paid men working by the side of skilled men, toward moving into related areas hitherto neglected, and, finally, even toward including accessible workers wholly unconnected with the main jurisdictions.

Part of the expansionist logic was simply opportunistic. Men who would pay dues could be had for the taking. Thus the explanation of a vice president of the butchers' union: "I couldn't see much future in just working on Meat Cutters and Packing House Workers, so I started on a campaign on the Creamery, Poultry, and Egg Houses."[31] For some union leaders, especially of the younger generation, more membership provided its own justification. Economic change, as always, played a part in reshaping jurisdictional interests. The Teamsters, for example, covered only local delivery drivers at the start of the thirties. During that decade, intercity trucking became a major industry: ton-mile traffic tripled between 1935 and 1941.[32] Although President Dan Tobin preferred to hold to the specialized local drivers—the so-called crafts—younger leaders pushed the union into this immense field, which employed more than a million men in 1941. In this instance, expansion promised added strategic advantages for the existing membership. In other cases, industrial change made growth necessary for defensive reasons. The butchers' union, which had limited itself in the retail field to meat cutters, began to organize food clerks, partly to protect the skilled men from changes growing out of the chain-store system and the self-service supermarket. The defensive reasons for expansion derived less, however, from economic developments than from the challenge of the C.I.O.

In 1934 the International Association of Machinists received jurisdiction over aircraft workers. At first the union acknowledged the rights of other organizations to men of their trades in the plants. By 1938, the I.A.M. was battling

[31] David Brody, *The Butcher Workmen: A Study of Unionization* (Cambridge, Mass., 1964), p. 248.

[32] Galenson, *CIO Challenge,* p. 472.

the C.I.O. for the aircraft workers and organizing "on the only basis that could be successful and that is, taking in all mechanics. . . . If this method is interfered with, the Machinists could not continue to organize in this industry." So, ironically, competition from the C.I.O. made this most stubborn opponent of industrial unionism in 1935 almost immediately an industrial union in some areas. By 1952, over a third of the Machinists' membership was classified as production workers, and the next year the union dropped entirely the distinction in membership between journeymen and others. It had cut loose entirely from its craft union origins.[33]

To avert the C.I.O., A.F. of L. unions moved also into neglected related fields. The United Brotherhood of Carpenters, for example, had successfully laid claim to the entire wood industry before World War I, but, despite greater capacity than any other union for effective action in the pre-New Deal period, this powerful craft union had actually not bothered about the woodworkers. When organization began almost spontaneously in the northwest during the N.R.A., the Carpenters accepted the woodworkers reluctantly as second-class participants in the organization. ("B" membership, involving lower dues, fewer benefits, and restricted political rights, was a standard way of handling new groups incorporated into A.F. of L. unions.) As soon as the C.I.O. invaded the Pacific lumber industry, that indifference faded: the woodworkers could not be permitted to organize independent of the Carpenters. A union fight of unparalleled violence and intensity ensued, even involving a naval battle between A.F. of L. and C.I.O. boats patrolling the waters around the sawmills.[34] As the C.I.O. expanded beyond the original basic industries, other A.F. of L. unions were likewise prompted to enter related fields: thus, initially to forestall the C.I.O., the Teamsters began to take in warehousemen; the Electricians, utility workers; the construction trades, residential building workers.

[33] *Ibid.*, p. 507; Mark Perlman, *The Machinists: A New Study of American Trade Unionism* (Cambridge, Mass., 1961), pp. 93, 212.

[34] Christie, *Empire in Wood*, chs. VIII, XIX, XX; Galenson, *CIO Challenge*, ch. XI.

The expansion of A.F. of L. unions grew, finally, from the discovery of special organizing advantages. Success was rarely forthcoming at the core of mass production industry. The C.I.O. excelled at organizing the great plants, the large industrial centers, the major firms, the points where the task was to win rank and file support and then utilize the democratic procedures of the Wagner act to acquire representational rights. But there remained a vast field outside or peripheral to the mass production sector that was susceptible to—indeed, better suited to—the tactics of the A.F. of L. unions. For one thing, they tended to have a decentralized structure. The local unions, established everywhere, gave access to the dispersed parts of the economy. And, with a large degree of autonomy, the locals had both the means and desire to carry on organizing work. A further superiority became apparent after the great surge of organization. The decentralized A.F. of L. nationals did not have to service their locals intensively, as did C.I.O. industrial unions, and so had a greater part of their income free for organizing work. Local vitality, although rarely noticed, made a steady contribution of immense importance to the growth of the A.F. of L.

As important as decentralization was the strategic power available to some organizations. Once the Teamsters began to incorporate highway drivers, the union held a powerful weapon for coercive organizing. By compelling union trucking firms not to transfer freight to non-union lines, the Teamsters could force the latter to recognize them and so extend their organization with vast efficiency. Using "leapfrog organizing" (as they called it), the Teamsters in the late thirties jumped from Chicago to St. Louis and Joplin, Missouri, from Minneapolis to Kansas City and Omaha. The intercity trucking industry was thus swiftly organized. The same leverage was then applied to local truckers, and finally to a wide range of businesses dependent on truck deliveries. The Teamsters rendered vital help to unions organizing retail stores, bakeries, laundries, and a host of small manufacturing plants, and then gradually began to retain these diversified groups within the organization. "Once you have the road men," Jimmy Hoffa boasted, "you can have the local cartage, and once you have the local cartage, you can get anyone you want."[35]

While not so strategically located as the Teamsters, other A.F. of L. unions made good use of pressure tactics. In the fierce fight for the northwest lumber industry, the Carpenters refused to handle wood produced in C.I.O. plants. "Why don't [the C.I.O. leaders] admit that a union is strong or weak depending on its power to boycott efficiently?" crowed the United Brotherhood. The boycott enabled the Carpenters to recapture a substantial part of the Pacific industry, despite lack of popularity and resourceful opposition from the C.I.O. union.[36] The retail branch of the A.F. of L. butchers' union exerted the same kind of pressure on meat processing plants, and to some extent so did other craft unions moving into manufacturing fields. Although the techniques varied immensely, and included collusion as well as force, strategic A.F. of L. unions followed the essential approach of concentrating their organizing efforts on employers no less than on workers. Notwithstanding the fact that it conflicted with the democratic policy of the Wagner act to give workers a free choice on union representation, this tactic was fostered by many developments in the thirties, above all by legal sanctions permitting organizational picketing and the secondary boycott.

So the favorable environment evoked from the labor movement two patterns of growth. The dramatic response involved the creation of industrial unions for the basic industries. Some old-line unions meanwhile evolved into diversified organizations especially effective at reaching the less accessible workmen outside the mass production sector of the economy. These two approaches had never been entirely distinct, and they overlapped even more as the industrial unions exhausted their main fields. Together, they lifted the labor movement to the level of eighteen million members by 1955 (three million outside the A.F. of L. and C.I.O.). American trade unionism had found within itself capacities for expansion unanticipated in the trying years prior to the great depression and the New Deal.

[35] Ralph and Estelle James, *Hoffa and the Teamsters* (Princeton, N.J., 1965), p. 100 and *passim*.

[36] Christie, *Empire in Wood*, p. 302.

In the end, this analysis returns to its starting point. Professor Barnett had foreseen a diminishing future for the labor movement in 1932. During recent years, his gloomy words have found an echo among union experts. In 1953 the labor editor of *Fortune,* Daniel Bell, announced that "U.S. labor has lost the greatest single dynamic any movement can have—a confidence that it is going to get bigger. Organized labor has probably passed its peak strength." Although his argument was disputed at the time, Bell's prediction proved to be shrewd and accurate. During the rest of the fifties the increase of union membership—at an average rate of roughly one hundred thousand per year—was not great enough even to maintain the unions' share of the total labor force.[37] Trade unionism seemed to be

[37] Daniel Bell, "The Next American Labor Movement," *Fortune,* XLVII (April, 1953), 204. Irving Bernstein took issue with Bell in a fine article which, while it could not negate the accuracy of Bell's prediction, did demonstrate conclusively the lack of correlation between union growth and the major indices of economic activity ("The Growth of American Unions," *American Economic Review,* XLIV [June, 1954], 301–18). In a subsequent article in 1961, Bernstein argued that the labor movement had actually turned in a creditable growth performance since the end of World War II. He attempted to answer the "saturationist" position that labor had reached the limit of the organizable part of the economy by pointing to the growth of unions in the non-manufacturing sector and by arguing that women, the South, agriculture, and white-collar work should not be written off as impervious to trade unionism. And he presented a new series that showed greater growth since 1945 than had appeared in earlier statistics:

Year	Membership	% of Civilian Labor Force
1945	13,379,000	24.8
1946	13,648,000	23.7
1947	14,845,000	24.7
1949	14,960,000	24.1
1950	14,751,000	23.4
1951	16,211,000	25.8
1952	16,730,000	26.6
1953	17,884,000	28.0
1954	17,757,000	27.5
1955	17,749,000	27.0
1956	18,477,000	27.4
1957	18,430,000	27.1
1958	18,081,000	26.3
1959	18,452,000	26.6
1960	18,607,000	26.2

hardening. Its ideas lacked freshness, its policies popular appeal. Age crept up even on those new-style leaders like Walter Reuther, who were raised in the great upheaval of the thirties. When Congressional investigation revealed undemocratic internal politics and widespread corrupt practices, the final signs of labor's declining vitality seemed clear. Recent criticisms recall the harshness of pre-New Deal observers of trade unionism.

Obviously, the movement has not come full circle. Organized labor is incomparably stronger today than it was thirty-five years ago. Powerful labor unions now share in the basic decisions that govern the economy. The A.F. of L.-C.I.O. exerts an influence in politics beyond anything envisaged by Samuel Gompers. In its internal affairs, organized labor has become more flexible and realistic. It would be hard to imagine the A.F. of L.-C.I.O. being held back, as was the A.F. of L. before 1935, by rigid notions of jurisdictional rights and trade autonomy. And the organizing techniques devised by A.F. of L. unions continue to have a significant measure of success in non-manufacturing areas.

Yet as a whole, the labor movement finds itself at a standstill. Despite the important differences, the situation today has an underlying similarity with that before the depression. Growth has stopped because organized labor has again run into an unfavorable environment. And, as earlier, the movement is stymied. Its greater strength notwithstanding, it still lacks the capacity to change the adverse environment. It cannot forestall the new technology that is cutting into its base in many fields; at best, it hopes to protect those of its members caught by change. It cannot reverse legislative and court decisions, beginning with the Taft-Hartley act, that have taken away some key advantages. It can do little to change the circumstances that make

Although these statistics do show an impressive increase of 4.5 million members between 1945 and 1953, primarily during the Korean War, since then Bernstein's figures show an average increase of only one hundred thousand a year, and the percentage of union members in the labor force slipped by almost two points ("The Growth of American Unions, 1945–1960," *Labor History*, II [Spring, 1961], 131–57).

the major unorganized areas—the South, agriculture, white-collar work—unresponsive to trade unionism. Nor, on the other hand, has the labor movement shown much greater ability to alter itself in ways that would permit it to grow *within* the contemporary environment than it had before the depression. As earlier, organized labor has found no answer to adversity.

The foregoing line of analysis does suggest two predictions beyond what Professor Barnett saw in 1932. Should the environment become more favorable—possibly as a result of racial progress in the South, new labor patterns in agriculture, automation in white-collar fields, or, more dramatically, from political or economic upheaval—the labor movement would show itself able to seize the opportunity. It is equally probable that, should another breakthrough occur, trade unionism would not depart from the basic direction charted by Samuel Gompers any more than the movement did in the thirties. By drawing these two lessons from recent labor history, of course, a third is ignored: namely, not to make predictions and so to avoid being found in error, as is the case with Professor Barnett here, by future historians.

II

THE PATTERN OF MODERN AMERICAN NATIONAL POLITICS

by William E. Leuchtenburg

The paradox of the two-party system in the United States is that it has been so feeble and so durable. The frailty of American parties is notorious. A congeries of state and local organizations, the national party has found it difficult to impose order on its components. An institution without members, the "party" has no clearly defined corpus. Called on to appeal to a heterogeneous people in a continental empire, the major parties have been doctrinally diffuse.

Yet the American party system has the most ancient lineage in the world. Both the Republicans and their senior rivals, the Democrats, are more than a century old. As Maurice Duverger has pointed out, "In 1850 no country in the world (except the United States) knew political parties in the modern sense of the word." Furthermore, the attachment of voters to the two major parties has been remarkably constant. Save for the special case of the 1912 Progressives, no third party since the Civil War has won more than one fifth of the presidential vote.

Even more striking is the pattern of alternation of power. Political reins do not change hands every four years. Instead, one party predominates for a generation or more, until some cataclysmic event breaks its hold. In the past century, there have been two cataclysms: the Civil War and the Great Depression. Each shaped the politics of the ensuing period, and reverberations from both these upheavals continue to be felt.

A child born in Detroit today will go to school, study the issues of modern America, listen thoughtfully to the claims of both parties, and when he comes of age will walk into a voting booth and pull down all the Democratic levers—because he is part of a culture shaped by the breadlines and the picket lines of the nineteen thirties. A child born in the Adirondacks today will go to school, attend civics classes, give a fair hearing to both parties, wonder in his own mind what he is going to do, and when the time comes will cast a solid vote for the Republican Party—because of a quarrel over the Kansas-Nebraska Act about which he may be only dimly aware or about which he may never even have heard.

To be sure, elections are not tightly locked into the matrix of tradition. The outcome of no given contest is predetermined. In a particular year, enough voters may temporarily cross party lines to decide the result. V. O. Key has estimated the number of switchers in recent years at as high as one fifth. Moreover, the electorate is constantly being altered by an influx of young voters or of inconsistent or independent voters with no firm party identification.

Nor are parties as homogenized as the stereotypes suggest. Although both Democrats and Republicans draw support from all sections and groups, one party is likely to have a greater following than the other in particular regions, nationalities, religions, and classes. At different times in the past, too, the parties have diverged on questions of national policy. Since, on those occasions, candidates have offered meaningful options, the act of voting has been more rational than some rigidly deterministic accounts have implied. It is true that the United States has not been torn by questions like clericalism, monarchism, or caste conflict, yet disagreements over issues have often separated the two parties. These disputes have sometimes reflected the demands of the dissimilar components of the parties, sometimes the parties' own institutional interests.

Still, no observation about voting behavior in the United States is more pertinent than that of the persistent attachments formed by the great majority of Americans to one or the other of the two major parties. Political socialization takes place at an early age, and partisan disposition is acquired with table manners. Although party loyalties may wither over time, they are often passed on from generation to generation. Once an eruption has catapulted a party into a position of predominance, it is likely to remain there for a long period.

The Era of Republican Supremacy

From 1860 to 1932 the Republican Party dominated national politics. During those seventy-two years, not a single Democrat entered the White House with 50 per cent of the vote. Grover Cleveland and Woodrow Wilson, the only Democrats to capture the presidency in this period, each won twice with less than a popular majority. Otherwise, it was an age of Republican success. Of the thirty-six sessions of Congress in this era, the Republican Party controlled the House twenty-three times, the Senate thirty-one.

The Republicans could present themselves as the party of the Union, as an institution which had led the country through a victorious war to save the republic, guided by Abraham Lincoln, the nation's savior and martyr. Republicans seized on the rapidly growing legend of Abraham Lincoln as Christ figure, martyred by evil men on Good Friday, on the brink of his triumph over the Antichrist. As late as the nineteen thirties in Muncie, Indiana, a minister declared in a Lincoln's Birthday sermon: "Lincoln was sent by God to save the nation as clearly as Christ was sent to save the race."

By denouncing the Democrats as the party of treason, Republicans sought to win northern voters to the Grand Old Party which had stood by the flag. For a generation the Republican slogan was "Vote the Way You Shot." Robert Morss Lovett recalls: "The first reference to politics that I remember was the question, 'Who're *you* for?' And a boy's reply, 'Hayes and Wheeler.' The long contest over the election was settled for us in favor of Hayes by the pronouncement of Grandpa. 'He has a bullet in him.' "

Of the two events which have shaped modern American politics—the struggle over slavery and the Great Depression—the dispute over slavery was more important in establishing the topography of American politics. By the end of Reconstruction, the political maps with which we have been familiar in the twentieth century had been drawn, featuring the pre-eminence of the Democrats in the South and in the northern cities and the fealty to the Republicans in the rural sections of the northern and central states.

Decades later, the Republican coalition still showed the imprint of sectional divisions over slavery. In the South, pockets of Unionism during the Civil War persisted as enclaves of Republicanism; in 1936, mountain Republicans of the southern Appalachians voted 89 per cent for Landon. In the old northwest, Ohio, Indiana, and Illinois were delicately balanced between a Republican sector in the North into which anti-slavery New Englanders had migrated and a Democratic sector in the South where Virginians and Kentuckians had settled. (In *Midwest Politics,* John H. Fenton reported in 1966 that the two parties in Ohio, Indiana, and Illinois still diverged "along Civil War lines" a century after that conflict ended.) Since few of the southern migrants got as far north as Michigan, Wisconsin, and Minnesota, these states were one-party Republican sanctuaries from the Civil War until the Great Depression.

As yet another consequence of the Civil War, the Republicans held the allegiance of Negro voters. The Negro leader Frederick Douglass said: "The Republican Party is the ship; all else is the sea." Since Negroes were concentrated in the South, their loyalty to the GOP proved relatively unimportant in the late nineteenth century, when the Southern Negro was ruthlessly disfranchised. But in the years after World War I, when hundreds of thousands of Negroes moved north, Negro ballots bolstered Republican candidates until the New Deal.

The Republican heartland was New England and the New England belt of migration, embracing areas like upper New York State and the Western Reserve, sweeping west to Kansas, and jumping the Rockies to Oregon. Since the New

England belt was overwhelmingly rural, old stock, and Protestant, GOP programs bore the mark of such regional doctrines as temperance, nativism, and anti-Catholicism. Republicanism flourished in the centers of Prohibitionism, and it had been born, in part, out of the anti-alien, anti-Catholic Know-Nothing movement of the eighteen fifties. In presidential campaigns in which religious issues have been involved, the Republican Party has always been aligned with those forces more favorable to a Protestant outlook, while the Democrats have been the only major party to nominate a Catholic (in 1928 and 1960) for the presidency. At a time when most of the country was rural and much of the electorate came from Protestant Anglo-Saxon stock, the composition of the GOP was a source of power. But each boat that docked at an Atlantic port with a cargo of immigrants from Ireland or southern and eastern Europe raised a new threat to the Party.

Perhaps the greatest advantage the Republicans held was that people accepted them as the natural ruling party in America. As Mr. Dooley once observed: "Histhory always vindicates the dimmycrats, but niver in their lifetime. They see the thruth first, but the throuble is that nawthin' is iver officially thrue till a raypublican sees it." To a considerable extent, the Republicans obtained for themselves an aura of legitimacy, so that many men regarded the Party as representing all that was best in American culture. In a speech on the Republicans' fiftieth anniversary, John Hay wryly attributed to the Party "all the good things of the half century, except, possibly, the introduction of antiseptic surgery."

One Republican senator, asked to explain the difference between the parties, replied:

> The men who do the work of piety and charity in our churches, the men who administer our school system, the men who own and till their own farms, the men who perform skilled labor in the shops, the soldiers, the men who went to war and stayed all through, the men who paid the debt and kept the currency sound and saved the nation's honor, the men who saved the country in war and have made it worth living in peace, commonly and as a rule, by the natural law of their being find their places in the Republican party. While the old slave-owner and

> slave-driver, the saloon keeper, the ballot box stuffer, the Ku Klux Klan, the criminal class of the great cities, the men who cannot read or write, commonly and as a rule, by the natural law of their being, find their congenial place in the Democratic party.

With their great strength in the New England belt, which prided itself on its role as the guardian and carrier of culture, the Republicans thought of themselves as the party of the better elements and the spokesmen for the values of Emerson and Whittier. Throughout the New England belt, the Republicans were the gentry, the squires, the professional men—the lawyers, the doctors, the ministers, the professors. With the exception of the South, fewer of the respectable, substantial people of the country were Democrats than Republicans. Fred Howe recalls: "There was something unthinkable to me about being a Democrat—Democrats, Copperheads and atheists were persons whom one did not know socially. As a boy I did not play with their children."

In the eyes of Republicans, Clinton Rossiter has noted, the Democrats have been the party of heresy and even of treason, from Clement Vallandigham in the eighteen sixties to Alger Hiss in the nineteen forties. As the party of the "enemy," the Democrats were at a severe disadvantage in the aftermath of the Civil War. Carl Schurz remarked: "There is no heavier burden for a political party to bear, than to have appeared unpatriotic in war."

Despite these liabilities, the Democrats showed surprising resilience. By 1876, only eleven years after Appomattox, they had outpolled the Republicans in a presidential election. Once the troops were withdrawn from the South, that entire region moved into the Democratic camp. By 1880 the Democrats were boasting of a new political phenomenon: the Solid South. That year, their presidential nominee carried every southern state, as Democratic candidates were to do in almost every election thereafter.

Nor was Democratic power confined to the South. The Democrats had always been much less of a sectional party than the Republicans. In 1860 Breckinridge had attracted more votes in New England alone than Lincoln was able to poll in the South and border states combined. After the war the Democrats prospered in old Jacksonian sections of New England, in the belt of southern migration in the Midwest, and, above all, in the northern cities. From 1868 to 1892, the Republicans failed to win more than 35 per cent of the vote of the nation's ten largest cities.

The mainstays of the Democratic Party in the northern cities were the recent immigrants, and especially the Irish-Americans. It was regarded as axiomatic that any good Irish Catholic was a Democrat: "Have you heard the news? John Danaher has become a Republican." "It can't be true. I saw him at mass just last Sunday." Resentful of the nativism and anti-Catholicism associated with the GOP, Catholics found a home in the Democratic Party. (As late as 1960, of the Catholic members of Congress more than 80 per cent were Democrats.) Chiefly workingmen, Irish Catholics felt a class antipathy to the Republican squirearchy in states like Massachusetts. Concentrated in cities, they came into political and cultural conflict with the rural Protestant supporters of the Republican Party. Although foes of the Irish such as French-Canadians and British immigrants flocked to the GOP, other ethnic groups shared the allegiance of the Irish to the Democratic Party.

The Democrats proved potent enough to establish, for a period of two decades, beginning in 1874, a politics of almost even division. The 55.6 per cent of the presidential vote polled by the Republicans in 1872 had been cut to 47.9 per cent in 1876. The GOP failed to win a majority of the popular vote in any of the five presidential elections from 1876 to 1892. In only one of these contests did they gain even a plurality, and that by less than 0.1 per cent. In three of the five elections, the difference in popular vote between the two major party candidates was smaller than 1 per cent.

In these years of party equilibrium, no issue of consequence divided the parties. Those topics that were aired—currency, the tariff—arrayed antagonists within parties rather than between them. Civil rights, once a meaningful question, was by 1877 no longer a genuine political issue, as the North acquiesced in the disfranchisement and exploitation of the southern Negro. In April, 1877, *The Nation* asserted: "The negro will disappear from the field of northern politics. Henceforth the nation, as a nation, will have nothing more to do with him." Although minor parties like the Greenbackers were sometimes able to interpose themselves in policy matters, only rarely did politicians concern themselves with the implications of industrialization.

At a time when the United States played only a walk-on part on the world stage, differences over foreign policy were too insignificant to have much impact on party alignments. But disputes over foreign affairs did offer an occasion for rhetorical ruses to lure ethnic voters. Both parties appealed to Anglophobes by twisting the lion's tail. For the past century Republicans have tried to pick off Irish votes by stressing overseas issues. They have denounced Democratic presidents as either indifferent to the cause of Irish independence or as pawns of Downing Street, from the Republicans' bid to the Fenians in the eighteen sixties through their assault on Wilson and the League in 1919 down to their attack on Franklin Roosevelt's support of Britain in 1940. (More recently, anti-communism has taken the place of baiting the British.)

In the eighteen nineties this issueless politics of dead center came to an end. With the passage of time, the divisions of the Civil War lost their immediacy. Although even a century later politics would bear the mark of the war alignments, by the nineties a new generation of Americans had no memory of that fratricidal conflict. The tidal waves of immigration yielded peasants from Mittel-europa who were not stirred by recollections of Shiloh and Antietam. The admission of western states (six of them entered the Union in a rush in 1889 and 1890) introduced, as new counters in the electoral game, units which had not experienced directly the agony of disunion. All these developments jeopardized traditional alignments.

Even more important was the rise of the Populists, the only third party to break into the electoral column in the period from 1860 to 1912. By advocating such measures as the direct election of U.S. senators and government ownership of railroads, the Populists focused attention on a new set of issues. By uniting class animosities, sectional cleavages, and urban-rural resentments in a single movement, Populism threatened the pre-eminence of the two major parties. Around the talisman of silver grouped the rebellious farmers of the South and the Middle Border and the mining interests of the mountain states.

Only one element was missing: a national experience that would cut voters loose from their old moorings. Two months after Grover Cleveland began his second term of office, the country was plunged into the panic of 1893. Fifteen thousand businesses collapsed in a single year. In New York money virtually disappeared. Henry Adams wrote of the impact on State Street: "Men died like flies under the strain, and Boston grew suddenly old, haggard, and thin." Not until the crash of 1929 was the country to see a depression which caused so much misery as that of 1893. In the winter of 1894, one hundred thousand men walked the streets of Chicago looking for jobs. The British journalist William Stead wrote: "Like the frogs in the Egyptian plague, you could not escape the tramps, go where you could."

In the nineties all the institutions for class amelioration seemed to buckle. Many predicted that the United States would adopt the Old World model of a politics of outright class antagonism with a farmer-labor party as a permanent instrumentality. As it turned out, neither the Populists nor the Bryanite Democrats were able to build a movement with a wide enough electoral base. Populism in the East was always a negligible force (in 1892, the Populists got fewer votes in the Northeast than did the Prohibitionists) and the eastern worker distrusted the Bryan Democrats. Nor did the tribunes of agrarian unrest make much headway in the Old Northwest. In 1892, the Populists captured only one county north of the Ohio and east of the Mississippi, and in 1896, the Corn Belt backed McKinley.

Instead of turning to a farmer-labor party or a Bryanized Democracy, the country revenged itself on the Democrats as the party in power during hard times by re-establishing Republican supremacy. The Democrats were stigmatized as the authors of depression and the Republicans were lauded as the custodians of prosperity, reputations that would be drummed home by GOP speakers from the full dinner pail appeal of McKinley in 1900 through the two cars in every garage campaign of Hoover in 1928. The combination of the panic and the Bryanite campaign convinced many that the Democrats were untrustworthy managers of business affairs. Walter Lippmann later recalled: "I was a child of four during the panic of '93, and Cleveland has always been a sinister figure to me. His name was uttered with monstrous dread in the household. Then came Bryan, an ogre from the West, and a waiting for the election returns of 1896 with beating heart. And to this day I find myself with a subtle prejudice against Democrats that goes deeper than what we call political conviction."

The elections of the nineties demolished the politics of equilibrium and restored Republican predominance. In twenty-four states in 1894 the Democrats failed to elect a single member of the House. The Republicans held on to their traditional areas in the New England belt and added two other sectors which gave them a decisive advantage. One was the northern cities which swung into the GOP column, where they remained until the nineteen twenties. The other was the Midwest, which, as a consequence of urbanization and the diversification of farming, now had more in common with the Republicanism of the Northeast than the Bryanism of the Great Plains.

For the next generation, the Republicans not only won national elections but won them by substantial margins. From 1894 to 1930, the democrats triumphed in only three Congressional elections. Although the Democrats had captured the House eight of ten times from 1874 to 1894, the Republicans controlled both houses of Congress from 1894 to 1910. In some twenty northern and western states, the GOP, the party of free soil and good times, was almost as certain of victory as the Democrats were in the South. Of the fourteen states which entered the Union after 1860, only one supported the Democrats in the majority of elections up to 1932.

This age of Republican supremacy was interrupted just once—when the discord over progressivism severed the Party. The agitation of the Progressives not only introduced a new set of policy concerns but also temporarily affected the alignment of the parties. For the Democrats, progressivism was a boon. After oscillating between a Bryan wing with little urban appeal and a Cleveland wing which was unattractive to the South and West, the Democrats made the most of their opportunity to develop a new stance under progressive leaders like Woodrow Wilson, who found a national following. For the Republicans, progressivism proved divisive and expensive; in 1910, as insurgents battled with Taft regulars, the Democrats rebounded. In 1912, when Teddy Roosevelt led his Bull Moose faction out of the GOP to form the Progressive Party and Eugene Debs polled nearly a million votes on the Socialist ticket, Wilson slipped into the presidency although he received only 42 per cent of the vote. Four years later, he won re-election by a narrow margin in a campaign in which he combined the appeals of peace and progressivism.

Wilson's triumph in 1916 revealed a new phenomenon in American politics: foreign policy, for the first time, had a pivotal importance for party fortunes. Even the Spanish-American War had not had much influence on party conflict because the imperialism issue was blurred in 1900, although some voters, then and later, were attracted or appalled by Teddy Roosevelt's bellicosity. By 1916, foreign affairs had become paramount in deciding the way in which many voters would cast their ballots. Although the Republicans and Progressives had reunited, Wilson still managed to win. His record in his first term and his posture as the peace candidate not only gained him re-election but opened the possibility that the Democrats might shortly become the new majority party. Yet these same foreign policy concerns spelled Wilson's undoing. The antagonisms engendered by the war and the controversy over the League of Nations ended the brief Democratic interlude.

In 1920 Warren Harding scored the greatest victory in the history of the Republican Party. He captured every state in the North and West, every county but one in New England, every borough of New York City. He even broke the Solid South by carrying Tennessee. His margin was swollen by the increment of the vote of women. At the Democratic convention in 1920, when the woman-suffrage plank was read, the band struck up "Oh, You Beautiful Doll." That summer, Tennessee, the thirty-sixth state, ratified the Nineteenth Amendment, and millions of women cast ballots that fall. In 1920, as in subsequent elections, the main partisan benefits of the expansion of woman suffrage were enjoyed by the Republicans.

In all sections, foreign policy issues took their toll of the Democrats. On the Pacific coast, where Harding won every county, voters who had backed Wilson in 1916 for keeping the country out of war punished the Democrats for failing to make good on the implied pledge. In the Northeast, the Democrats were hurt by the resentment of ethnic groups over Wilson's overseas policy. Italian-Americans were angry about Fiume, Germans about the war itself. The Irish, who stayed away from the polls in droves, execrated both the war and the peace as British conspiracies. As early as March, 1919, one Irish leader warned: "If the Democratic Party indorses Wilson's actions, we have not as much show of electing a Democratic President next year, as Villa has of going to Heaven."

For the Democrats the situation in the twenties seemed hopeless. The combination put together by the Republicans in the nineteenth century and rebuilt in the World War I era appeared unbeatable. The Democrats, split between urban and rural elements on issues like prohibition and the Ku Klux Klan, often generated more interest in quarreling among themselves than in mounting effective opposition to the Republicans, who claimed they had a mandate for isolationism and conservatism. In 1924, the Democratic presidential candidate, John W. Davis, carried only twelve states in the whole country, not one outside the South. In some states he ran behind the third-party candidate, the Progressive Robert M. La Follette. The Democrats were demoralized. Their national headquarters in Washington, observed a reporter, were "as Romish catacombs or Pompeian atriums, elegantly preserved but destitute."

After the election, one of the younger Democrats questioned Party leaders to find how they accounted for the Party's sad state and to inquire what should be done. Congressman Henry Rainey of Illinois, later to be Speaker, replied: "We can do nothing except wait for the Republican party to blow up." It would require a depression to change the Party's fortunes. A Fort Wayne publisher agreed. He did not see how the Party could regain power "except the country have disaster." The young Democrat who posed these questions was also inclined to take the long view. "Frankly," Franklin D. Roosevelt told a reporter, "I do not look for a Democratic president until after the 1932 election."

The Upheaval of the Great Depression

When Herbert Hoover won the presidency by an emphatic margin in November, 1928, the Republican Party was at its zenith. Hoover not only swept almost all of the North and West but cut deeply into the once-solid South. Less than a year later, the Wall Street crash signaled the beginning of a prolonged depression which was to upset the balance between the major parties. Just as the struggle over slavery detonated a political explosion that started a long period of Republican dominance, so the Great Depression marked the end of GOP supremacy and the emergence of the Democrats as the new majority party.

In 1932, Franklin D. Roosevelt captured forty-two of the forty-eight states. Hoover, who in 1928 had carried forty states, now won only six. It was the worst setback a Republican candidate had ever suffered in a two-party race. Since 1932 the Republicans have continued to bear the stigma of the Great Depression. A generation later, voters still thought of the GOP as the party of bad times, the instrument of the wealthy, an institution less qualified than the Democrats to cope with domestic problems. From 1932 to the present, the Republicans have controlled Congress for only four years.

The GOP has been reduced during much of this time to the remnants of its nineteenth-century empire in those states in the New England belt and the Great Plains where rural and small-town influence still predominates. From 1932 through 1964, only ten states have backed the Republicans a majority of the time. They are clustered in northern New England and in a constellation of central states bounded by Indiana on the east, Colorado on the west, North Dakota on the north, and Kansas on the south.

The 1932 election realigned voters' loyalties; the Democrats not only scored heavily among new voters but converted former Republicans to the Democratic Party. In the next four years, Roosevelt consolidated these gains through a series of enactments which brought tangible benefits. The Democrats thrived on "the politics of the deed": relief checks, C.C.C. jobs, insured bank deposits, homes saved from mortgage foreclosure. The federal government, once a remote institution, acted directly on the lives of individual Americans. In 1934, the Democrats reaped the political benefit when, instead of maintaining the tradition of losing seats in a midterm election, they expanded their delegations in both houses of Congress.

By 1936, Roosevelt had exploited the opportunity offered by the depression to create a new political coalition based on the masses in the great cities. The switch-over of metropolitan centers to the Democrats had begun in response to the appeal in 1928 of Al Smith, cynosure of the newer Americans in the cities. Smith was born in a tenement on the lower East Side. (As Jacob Javits recently remarked, "In New York State, that is like being born in a log cabin.") In 1928 Smith carried a multitude of ethnic wards by stunning margins—the French ward of Holyoke by over 84 per cent, a Jewish ward in Chelsea by 81 per cent, an Irish ward in South Boston by 90 per cent.

Roosevelt improved on Smith's performance in the cities, which since 1894 had been in the Republican column. While Smith won the cities by a slender margin, F. D. R. carried them overwhelmingly. In 1932, Roosevelt captured every metropolis in the Midwest, West, and South. The Democratic vote in Detroit jumped from 37 per cent in 1928 to 59 per cent in 1932, in Los Angeles from 29 to 60 per cent, in Dallas from 39 to 81 per cent. In 1936, F. D. R. did even better. Of the cities of one hundred thousand population or more, Roosevelt captured 104, Landon 2. He swept every ward in Pittsburgh, took New York City by the unbelievable plurality of 1,367,000, and carried traditionally Republican Philadelphia by the widest margin any Democrat had ever achieved in that city.

Roosevelt's urban coalition owed much to the ardent support of the newer ethnic groups, who were grateful for New Deal welfare measures and delighted with being granted "recognition." (The President appointed the first Italo-American ever named to a federal judgeship.) Even more impressive was the massive swing of Negro voters to the Democratic Party. As late as 1932, Negroes were tenaciously Republican. Cincinnati's heavily Negro Ward 16 gave Roosevelt less than 29 per cent of the vote. But in 1934 Negroes began to switch to the Democratic Party, and in 1936 F. D. R. carried Negro wards handsomely. Battered by the depression, which hit them especially hard, Negroes were gratified by New Deal welfare programs and drawn to an administration many of whose members were committed to equal rights. A Pennsylvania Negro, asked to explain his vote for the local Democrats, replied that he had seen President Roosevelt's picture: "Anybody that has that picture beside him can get my vote." A Republican ward leader complained: "I can beat the Democrats, but that damned Roosevelt has taken Lincoln's place."

Of exceptional importance in F. D. R.'s urban coalition was organized labor. "Labor," John L. Lewis asserted, "has gained more under President Roosevelt than any President in memory. Obviously it is the duty of labor to support Roosevelt 100 per cent in the next election." The decision of Lewis and of garment worker leaders like Sidney Hillman and David Dubinsky to work for the re-election of Roosevelt in 1936 broke precedent. In 1932, unions had made almost no contribution to the Roosevelt cause. The garment unions had backed the Socialist Norman Thomas, and Lewis had endorsed Hoover.

In 1936, the Democrats got over three-quarters of a million dollars from unions. Nearly half a million dollars came from the United Mine Workers alone. At the same time, the proportion of contributions from businessmen dropped sharply. As one political scientist noted, it was a "new chapter" in the history of the labor movement "when an organization of miners is the largest contributor to a major political party." The $770,000 which the Democrats received from unions in 1936 contrasted sharply with the $95,000 which was the grand sum donated by the national A.F. of L. to national campaigns in the preceding thirty years. Lewis's forces did an effective job, too, in getting out the workingman's vote for Roosevelt in 1936. Labor was decisive in swinging states like Pennsylvania to the Democrats.

Labor's support for F. D. R. riveted attention on the most significant political development of the Roosevelt years, the nationalizing of American politics. Class replaced section as the critical determinant of partisan disposition. To be sure, sectional alignments endured. The South remained solidly Democratic, and midwestern small towns continued to be redoubts of Republicanism. But there were marked changes. "Iowa will go Democratic," Senator Dolliver once said, "the year Hell goes Methodist." But since the New Deal upheaval, Iowa has gone Democratic almost as often as not. In old Republican bastions in northern industrial states like Rhode Island, class, ethnic loyalties, and the issues engendered by the New Deal proved more meaningful than the pull of past allegiances.

Of course, there had probably always been a tendency for men of wealth to gravitate to the Republicans, although the data before 1936 are too sparse to make this altogether clear. Yet before the "Roosevelt revolution," the impact of class on politics had been blurred; the Republican factory worker was a common phenomenon. Since 1936, however, the proportion voting Democratic has varied directly with socioeconomic status. By 1948, nearly 80 per cent of workers were voting Democratic, a percentage which, as Seymour Lipset has pointed out, is higher than that ever reported by left-wing parties in Europe.

This sharp cleavage was a result of the impact not only of the Great Depression but also of the New Deal, which established the Democrats as the party of big government and the workingman, the Republicans as the party of limited government and of business. This had not always been the case. In the late nineteenth century, the Republicans had been more closely identified with central government, the Democrats with states' rights. So suspicious had the Democrats been of centralized authority that one Republican Congresional leader asked in despair: "Are they but an organized No?" Although the period from Bryan to Wilson had altered the outlook of the Democrats, as late as the twenties little distinguished a Democratic presidential candidate like John W. Davis from a Republican candidate like Calvin Coolidge.

In the thirties, the parties became more polarized, and it became easier for voters to relate their decisions at the polls to policy preferences. Although the two parties remained loose confederations of local organizations, many of which had small interest in ideology, they could now be distinguished by their attitudes toward the welfare state. To denounce the New Deal, the Republicans employed the vocabulary of the old Jeffersonian Democrats. In Democratic councils the influence of the South, the refuge of traditional states' rights dogma, diminished; the repeal of the two thirds rule at the 1936 convention was one indication of its waning power. Intellectuals who favored increased government initiatives found a welcome in the Roosevelt administration and were drawn to the Democratic Party. With the urban interests of the northern states predominant, the Roosevelt coalition catered to voters who approved big government and appealed brashly to class sentiment.

As the 1936 campaign got under way, the note of class conflict sometimes reached a high pitch. At an excited night meeting at Forbes Field in Pittsburgh, a stern-faced Danton, State Senator Warren Roberts, spat out the names of the Republican oligarchs: Mellon, Grundy, Pew, Rockefeller.

The crowd greeted each name with a resounding "boo." "You could almost hear the swish of the guillotine blade," wrote one reporter afterwards. Then came Governor George Earle, their handsome Mirabeau, and he too churned up the crowd against the enemies of their class. "There are the Mellons, who have grown fabulously wealthy from the toil of the men of iron and steel . . . ; Grundy, whose sweatshop operators have been the shame and disgrace of Pennsylvania for a generation; Pew, who strives to build a political and economic empire with himself as dictator; the duPonts, whose dollars were earned with the blood of American soldiers; Morgan, financier of war." As he sounded each name, the crowd interrupted him with a chorus of jeers against the business leaders. Then the gates opened at a far corner of the park; a motorcycle convoy put-putted its way into the field, followed by an open car in which rode Franklin Delano Roosevelt, grinning and waving his hat, and the crowd, whipped to a frenzy, roared its welcome to their champion.

In January, 1936, Roosevelt guessed the Republicans would capture 216 electoral votes; in early August, he still gave them 191. In mid-September, Arthur Krock predicted: "The Republican party will poll a far larger popular and electoral vote than in 1932. Roosevelt's big majorities are over." Jim Farley was more optimistic. On November 2, he wrote the President: "I am still definitely of the opinion that you will carry every state but two—Maine and Vermont." The returns showed that Farley had hit it right on the nose. With 523 votes to Landon's 8, Roosevelt was re-elected by the greatest electoral margin in more than a century. Despite his class appeals, he had won sizable middle-class and business support. His rivals had been outclassed. The Socialists were decimated, and the followers of dissenters like Huey Long, the Reverend Charles Coughlin, and Dr. Francis Townsend had been drained off into the feckless Union Party. The Republican Congressional contingent had been reduced in the House from 267 in 1928 to 89 in 1936, from 56 to 17 in the Senate.

Roosevelt greeted news of the outcome with high glee. "I knew I should have gone to Maine and Vermont," the

President said gaily, "but Jim wouldn't let me." Never had a major party sustained so devastating a defeat as had the Republicans in 1936. William Allen White commented: "It was not an election the country has just undergone, but a political Johnstown flood." His policies vindicated, his opponents all but annihilated, Franklin Roosevelt had brought the Democratic Party to the crest of its fortunes.

The New Politics of Dead Center

After Roosevelt's smashing triumph in 1936, the Democrats seemed secure as the majority party for many long years to come. So powerful did the President's victory coalition appear that people seriously asked whether the Republican Party, like the Federalist Party of 1816, was not finished. Yet within two years of F. D. R.'s overwhelming success in 1936, the President had suffered a succession of defeats which ended hopes for a new era of reform. A series of developments—the costly fight over the Supreme Court, resentment at the sitdown strikes, and the recession of 1937–38—weakened the President's hold on his middle-class followers.

In the fall of 1937, southern Democrats and Republicans forged a conservative coalition that was to dominate American politics for the next generation. The coalition was not as monolithic as some writers made it seem. (One Ohio Congressman explained: "Sometimes I coalesce. Sometimes I don't.") Yet it was potent enough to kill some New Deal proposals and disembowel others. When in the summer of 1938 Roosevelt sought to "purge" the rebellious Democrats, the campaign fizzled. That fall, the Republican Party dealt the Roosevelt coalition another severe blow by picking up eighty-one seats in the House and eight in the Senate.

At this point, a new politics of dead center began. After the passage of the Fair Labor Standards Act in 1938, almost no innovative domestic legislation was adopted for the next quarter of a century. During that same period, neither party won at the polls the kind of margin that Roosevelt had commanded in his early years or that the Republicans had enjoyed even earlier. The New Dealers lacked the leverage in Congress to overcome the conservative coalition. Yet since most voters continued to identify with the Democrats, and since liberal Democrats controlled the White House through most of these years, conservatives were frustrated too. In the ensuing two decades, both conservatives and liberals tried to break this deadlock and impose their own policies; neither group had more than intermittent success.

For the next six years, Franklin Roosevelt continued to be the dominating figure in American politics, and the fortunes of the Democrats rode with him. In 1940 he won an unprecedented third term. By 1944 millions of Americans could not remember the time when there had been anyone in the White House but Roosevelt. The Chicago *Daily News* commented: "If he was good enough for my pappy and my grandpappy, he is good enough for me." Numerous stories speculated on the possibility that F. D. R. might reign forever. (In one story, a man who called on a stalwart Democrat who had just become the father of a baby boy suggested: "Maybe he'll grow up to be President." "Why, what's wrong with Roosevelt?" the father retorted.) In 1944, in the first wartime presidential election since 1864, Roosevelt won re-election to a fourth term, although the 62.5 per cent of the two-party vote he had polled in 1936 had fallen by 1944 to 53.8 per cent.

F. D. R.'s urban, lower-class coalition held up remarkably well in both campaigns. In 1940, voting in the cities broke sharply on class lines. Roosevelt captured wards in Minneapolis with rentals below forty dollars a month, lost those with higher rentals. Samuel Lubell concluded: "It was in the industrial centers that the Republican hopes were blacked out in factory smoke." In 1944 city ballots gave the President eight northern states with large electoral votes that would otherwise have gone to Dewey. As late as 1944, the leading reason people gave for supporting Roosevelt was that "he pulled us out of the depression."

Although the debate over intervention in World War II heightened the foreign policy concerns of the electorate, even in the 1940 campaign, as V. O. Key has pointed out, questions of domestic policy had far more influence on the vote.

Apprehension about foreign affairs turned voters in opposite directions. The Republicans gained among ethnic groups who were antagonized by Roosevelt's foreign policy—the Germans, the Italians, the Irish. But F. D. R. won support from those who favored militant opposition to the Axis and membership in a postwar association of nations. In the two most Jewish wards of Boston in 1944, the President received better than nine out of every ten votes. In Jewish precincts in Brooklyn, even Republican poll-watchers voted for Roosevelt.

Despite Roosevelt's triumphs, the politics of deadlock persisted. In Congress, the conservative coalition, which cemented its position during World War II, stymied the President on numerous occasions. In 1942, for the first time since 1928, GOP Congressional candidates received more votes than Democrats. The hard-core conservative delegation in Congress remained the fulcrum of the Republican Party, even though both in 1940 and 1944 the Party named presidential candidates from its more liberal and internationalist eastern wing. Under the leadership of men like Ohio's Robert Taft, Congress scuttled New Deal agencies and passed legislation to curb labor.

If the Republicans had continued to gain as they had during World War II, they would soon have won control both of Congress and the White House. The death of Roosevelt in 1945 removed the most formidable obstacle in their path. His successor, Harry Truman, had meager success in rallying liberals and labor to him, and conservatives disapproved his willingness to carry on New Deal reforms. Still more important were estrangements engendered by the problems of reconverting to a peacetime economy.

The 1946 elections coincided with popular resentment over a meat shortage, and the Republicans made the most of it. The GOP sang a chorus of "Horsemeat Harry," "To err is Truman," and "Don't shoot the piano player, he's doing the best he can." The shortage was "bad for the Democrats," observed one writer. "For as everybody knows, a housewife who cannot get hamburger is more dangerous than Medea wronged." Gallup polls showed that Truman's popularity had fallen from a peak of 87 per cent to a lowly

32 per cent. The President, on the advice of Party leaders, dropped out of the campaign altogether, and the Democrats played transcriptions of F. D. R.'s old campaign speeches over the radio instead.

In November, the Republicans won both houses of Congress; by swelling their holdings in the House to 246, they reached the high-water mark for this whole period. The returns indicated that the Roosevelt coalition was coming apart at the seams. In the cities the GOP had made gains among Negroes angered by the racism of southern Democrats, and Polish voters incensed at the postwar settlements. Truman had apparently been brutally repudiated. Democratic Senator William Fulbright urged him to name a Republican Secretary of State and resign from office to let the Republican succeed him (the Secretary of State was then next in line of succession); Democratic newspapers such as the Chicago *Sun* and the Atlanta *Constitution* backed Fulbright's proposal. Truman's re-election seemed out of the question. "The President," said the *United States News,* "is a one-termer."

Poor as Truman's prospects were after the 1946 elections, they became still bleaker when the Democratic Party splintered, and two factions broke away to form new parties. Vexed by a report by the President's Committee on Civil Rights and by the strong civil rights plank adopted at the 1948 Democratic convention, the "Dixiecrats" bolted to set up a new States Rights Party, with Governor J. Strom Thurmond as their presidential candidate. (That fall, the States Rights Democrats would win the electoral votes of four of the southern states.) While Dixiecrats were undercutting Truman's following on the right, left-wing critics of the President's foreign policy were imperiling his position in northern and western cities by creating yet another new party, the Progressive Party, with Henry Wallace as their presidential candidate.

Although these secessions seemed to assure a Republican victory in 1948, Truman upset all expectations in the most dramatic reversal of the century. His "give-em Hell, Harry" campaign against the "do-nothing, good-for-nothing 80th

Congress" attracted voters left cold by Dewey who, as one critic noted, sought the presidency with the "humorless calculation of a Certified Public Accountant in pursuit of the Holy Grail." In an election in which party identification was decisive, Truman had the advantage of running as the candidate of the majority party. Voters tempted to leave Democratic ranks were dissuaded by the performance of conservative Republicans in Congress and by Dewey's aloof posture. The GOP, it was said, had snatched defeat out of the jaws of victory.

Yet if the 1948 election once more confirmed the Democratic Party's hold on the White House, it also perpetuated the politics of dead center because Truman was not given enough support in Congress to push through such innovative proposals as national health insurance or civil rights legislation. His modest successes in his second term were largely confined to modifications of New Deal legislation. The end of the Truman era was a frustrating time in which the liberal tradition seemed exhausted and the conservative proposals irrelevant.

For a while the aridity of the struggle over domestic legislation contrasted perceptibly with the imaginativeness of United States foreign policy. The era of World War II had seen a radical shift in American thinking about international affairs. Although isolationism often emerged in new forms, such as Asia-Firstism, Congress over a period of years showed an exceptional willingness to experiment with new approaches toward other countries. From the Lend Lease Act of 1941 and the overwhelming vote to enter the United Nations in 1945 to the Marshall Plan of 1947, Congress compiled a brilliant record quite unlike its performance in the interwar era. Yet by the time the Point Four legislation had been pushed through in 1952, the period of innovation was giving way to the abrasions of the Cold War. Foreign aid programs were being subverted to military ends, and the rhetoric of the Cold War plagued thinking about domestic as well as foreign policy.

The Cold War also offered new opportunities to the Republicans, who were handicapped so long as politics revolved around the old questions of economic policy. Fortunately for the GOP, new issues were at hand. Only one month after Truman's surprise victory, Whittaker Chambers led two investigators to a pumpkin patch to pluck out microfilm of secret State Department documents. The Alger Hiss affair came at a time when a jolting set of events was undermining America's sense of security. Within a year after the excursion to the pumpkin patch, the State Department announced two dismaying pieces of news: China had fallen to the Communists and Russia had the Bomb. On February 9, 1950, two weeks after Hiss was sentenced to the penitentiary, Senator Joseph McCarthy launched a campaign based on the contention that whatever had gone wrong since 1945 was the result not of world events but of treason in Democratic administrations.

Much of the McCarthy indictment was based on dissatisfaction with Democratic policies toward Asia. When hostilities broke out in Korea in June, 1950, criticism of the Democrats intensified. No war the United States ever fought proved so unpopular as the Korean conflict. As casualties mounted, it seemed as though this struggle might go on forever, hopelessly, pointlessly, a limited war against an undefined enemy fought with no hope of absolute victory. A war no one wanted to fight, and no one knew how to end, it did untold damage to the Democratic Party. As the party in power during the third conflict in thirty-five years, the Democrats were open to the charge that they were the "war party." Foreign affairs, once of minor importance in party contests, now threatened to upset the balance of party alignments created by the upheavals of the Civil War and the Great Depression.

Discontent over Korea, the Communist scare, the deadlock in Congress, and tidings of corruption in Washington all raised the odds against the Democrats in 1952, but the Republicans still lacked a vote-getter. The logical candidate was "Mr. Republican," Senator Robert Taft, favorite of the more conservative, nationalist Republicans based in Congress and idol of Party officials in the hinterland. Seaboard leaders, dismayed by Taft's beliefs, doubted that the GOP, as a minority party, could risk running a representative Republican even in such a propitious year, and the polls confirmed their fears. So Senator Henry Cabot Lodge was dispatched to Paris to persuade Dwight Eisenhower, commanding general of the Allied Powers in Europe, to run. In a bitterly fought engagement, Eisenhower captured the GOP nomination from Taft.

A man who not only had no party record but who had been insulated from politics by years of military service, Eisenhower appealed to independents and recusant Democrats as a paladin who would bring clean government, dissipate the animosities of the Truman years, and go to Korea in quest of peace. The Republican formula in 1952 was, in Senator Karl Mundt's words, K_1C_2—Korea, communism, and corruption. Highly popular, Ike combined the martial virtues of a successful general with the benign countenance of a man of peace; he served to revivify Republican hopes much as Generals William Henry Harrison and Zachary Taylor had once served the Whigs.

In the 1952 elections, Eisenhower won a thumping victory. His opponent, Adlai Stevenson, failed to take a single state outside of the South and the border region. For the first time since 1928, a Republican candidate broke the Democratic hold on the Solid South. (In New Orleans, his supporters wore "J'aime Ike" buttons.) GOP gains in southern cities and northern suburbs suggested that 1952 had not only broken the long reign of the Democrats but had realigned voters to establish the Republicans as the new majority party.

Yet both survey data and the outcome of Congressional elections revealed that most voters continued to identify with the Democratic Party. Despite Eisenhower's topheavy margin in 1952, Republicans won a House majority of only eight seats and controlled the Senate by just one vote. In 1954 the Democrats recaptured control of both houses; for Ike's remaining six years in office, he had to work with a Congress run by the opposition party. In 1956, Eisenhower increased his plurality from the 55.4 per cent of the two-party vote of 1952 to 57.8 per cent; he gained an almost even split in the country's twelve largest cities and seized such

Democratic turf as Jersey City and Chicago. But in the teeth of Ike's 9.5 million majority, the Democrats again carried both houses of Congress; their candidates for the House outpolled their Republican rivals by 1.5 million votes. Not since Zachary Taylor had a President been elected without carrying at least one house.

In 1958, the Democrats built their greatest margin in Congress since F. D. R.'s heyday. Republican fortunes had sunk so low in the sixth year of Eisenhower's reign that the Party was left in command of only seven of the forty-eight state legislatures. Despite the almost six years in office of one of the most popular presidents in our history, the Republicans found themselves a minority party which was losing ground with every election. A Survey Research Center study in 1960 discovered that 54 per cent of respondents identified with the Democratic Party, and only 34 per cent with the Republicans. (Yet the gap was not quite as wide as it might seem, since Republicans were more likely to go to the polls.)

With a President of one party and a Congress of the other party, power was diffused. Paul David has written of the Eisenhower years: "The period was one of almost unprecedented ambiguity in regard to partisan responsibility for the conduct of the government." As a result of this division of authority, the President had to barter with the Democrats for whatever he wanted, and the liberals had to muster a two thirds vote to override Eisenhower's veto if they hoped to get legislation passed. The upshot was a period of middle-of-the-road government which was congruent with the quiescent spirit of the fifties. Adlai Stevenson conceded: "I agree that it is time for catching our breath; I agree that moderation is the spirit of the times."

By the end of the Eisenhower era, the United States had entered its third decade of the politics of dead center. While most voters identified with the Democrats, they gave their support to Eisenhower, a man who appeared to be "above party." (The former GOP Speaker, Joseph Martin, remarked of him: "*Republican* was a word that was not on the tip of his tongue.") Yet he shared enough of the beliefs of the Congressional Republicans to block attempts to advance new issues and to compel Democratic Congressional leaders like Lyndon Johnson to pursue a policy of compromise. With the President and Congress deadlocked, the Supreme Court was the only agency to break new ground, but its landmark decision in the Brown case lacked vigorous support from either the White House or Capitol Hill and met with widespread defiance. On the other hand, the conservatives and nationalists like the Senator from Arizona, Barry Goldwater, were frustrated in their efforts to repeal the New Deal and win approval for a more militant foreign policy. Although by 1960 publicists had begun to bemoan the lack of sense of national purpose, most of the country appeared content with the centrist politics of the past generation.

In 1960 both major parties chose presidential candidates who had been identified with the cautious politics of the fifties. Richard Nixon was often depicted as the hollow man of a synthetic society. John Kennedy, who had failed to take a bold stand on so critical an issue as McCarthyism, seemed representative of the unadventurous northern Democratic senators of the Eisenhower era, an impression that was reinforced when he chose Lyndon Johnson as his running mate.

Kennedy defeated Nixon after a campaign in which he began to sound the theme of the need to get America moving again, but in no sense could his victory be interpreted as a mandate for change. He won by only 0.2 per cent of the vote, and when the country elected the most conservative Congress in six years, it denied the President a working majority.

Kennedy brought to the White House a refreshing receptiveness to the need for change, but much of the time he was thwarted in his attempts to advance new policies. Although he undertook new initiatives in foreign affairs and drove through some significant domestic legislation, frequently he was balked by the conservative coalition in Congress and inhibited by his own awareness of his slim mandate. Some critics thought he was too sensitive to Jefferson's adage that "great innovations should not be forced on slender majorities." Yet the melancholy arithmetic of Congressional rollcalls could not be denied. When Medicare lost by four votes in the Senate, it had been opposed not only by almost every Republican but by twenty-one Democrats, every one of whom came from a southern or border state.

In the 1962 midterm elections, the Democrats came out better than any incumbent administration since 1934, but they still only succeeded in holding their own and thus preserving the stalemate. By the summer of 1963, everyone knew that Congress would recess without giving Kennedy either the civil rights or tax legislation he had requested. In mid-July, 1963, *Time* was tagging the Eighty-eighth Congress "the do-nothingest of modern times." On November 12, ten days before the President's death, the *New York Times* asserted: "Rarely has there been such a pervasive attitude of discouragement around Capitol Hill and such a feeling of helplessness to deal with it. This has been one of the least productive sessions of Congress within the memory of most of the members."

The Contours of Recent Politics

Although the Kennedy years saw the perpetuation of the politics of dead center, they also witnessed some dramatic departures. Kennedy's approach accentuated a hospitality to innovation—"the politics of modernity," to use John Roche's phrase—which helped make way for the changes wrought under Lyndon Johnson. In the sixties there have been three significant alterations—in the national mood, in the balance of power in Congress, and in the fortunes of the parties—which appear to indicate the advent of a new era in American politics.

Perhaps the most abrupt transformation has been in the national mood—a turn from the inactivity and indifference of the fifties to a lively interest in public affairs and social change in the sixties. The silent generation of the fifties has given way to the young activists of the sixties, who joined the Peace Corps or who risked their lives in the Deep South. The civil rights movement has not only bettered the position of the Negro but has had the ancillary effect of directing attention to neglected areas of American life. In part as a consequence of the civil rights tumult, books like Michael Harrington's study of poverty have found a ready response, and the rediscovery of the impoverished has become a national pastime. (The University of California offers a course called "Social Welfare X-427: Empathy with People in Poverty.") Submerged for a generation, a whole range of issues—from public welfare to metropolitan planning—has surfaced in the sixties.

The second metamorphosis of the sixties had been the end of the deadlock in Congress. To a degree under Kennedy, and much more markedly under Johnson, Congress has enacted the greatest spate of legislation since the New Deal. By passing such proposals as Medicare and federal aid to education, it adopted measures which had been advanced in the previous generation but had met with repeated defeat. After breaking the filibuster, civil rights advocates pushed through laws so drastic that they would have been unthinkable just a short time before. The rural-based conservative coalition, no longer powerful enough to decree the death of liberal bills, watched helplessly while Congress initiated the War on Poverty, terminated the 41-year-old national origins quota system on immigration, approved mass transit experiments, and created a cabinet-level Department of Housing and Urban Development, all of which testified to the rising importance of urban interests. By acceding to a multi-billion-dollar tax cut, Congress sanctioned "the quiet revolution" in economic policy by which the government rejected the old orthodoxies and purposefully fostered budget deficits to spur the economy. For a brief interval under Kennedy, Congress also agreed to novel gambits in foreign affairs: the Peace Corps, the Alliance for Progress, the Grand Design, the test ban treaty.

The third big change of the sixties has been the party upheaval highlighted by the election of 1964. That year the Republicans, who ever since 1936 had chosen a man of the center as their presidential candidate, broke tradition by naming Barry Goldwater, unmistakably a nominee of the right. Hero of those western nostalgic politicians who derided the eastern "Establishment," Goldwater once said: "Sometimes I think this country would be better off if we could just saw off the Eastern Seaboard and let it float out to sea." The Goldwater strategists claimed they could write off the populous Northeast and win with the support of the South and West by appealing to what was alleged to be a vast silent army of nationalist conservatives.

The 1964 elections exploded the theory of the silent vote and demonstrated the risk in a two-party system of nominating an uncompromising factionalist. Goldwater's demand for victory in the Cold War and his campaign to dismantle the federal government placed Johnson in the enviable position of being accepted as the "safe," more conservative candidate at the same time that he was advocating the Great Society. Johnson, who won by the biggest margin in history, restored the Democratic supremacy of the New Deal era in some areas and made new conquests for his party in others. For the first time since 1936, the Middle Border voted Democratic in a presidential contest, and the GOP lost such strongholds as suburban Westchester County, Republican in every two-party race since 1892.

Save for Arizona, Goldwater carried only the four Deep South states that had gone Dixiecrat in 1948, and Georgia, which had never before voted Republican. Attracted by Goldwater's racial views, the South, for the first time in history, provided the major electoral base of a GOP presidential nominee. Yet Goldwater actually did less well in the South than Eisenhower or Nixon. Carefully nurtured gains among southern moderates were wiped out as Virginia, Florida, and Tennessee, which had been Republican since 1948, returned to the Democratic column.

"The effect of the election," wrote one editor, "is to leave us with a crippled or deformed two-party system." For a generation the Republicans had been a minority party: in the period 1930 to 1964, they lost fifteen of seventeen Congressional elections, and the percentage of the electorate identifying itself as Democratic has steadily mounted. Goldwater's candidacy ruptured the Party and cost it its reputation as the "peace party." Composed of elements on the decline—northern European ethnic groups, rural and small-town provincials, entrepreneurial ideologues—the GOP seemed doomed to permanent minority status.

These three changes—the quickening of interest in public affairs, the ending of the legislative deadlock, and the restoration of Democratic supremacy—suggest that American politics has now entered a new phase. Yet there are indications that these may be only short-run phenomena. The 1964 elections lacked some of the characteristics of a genuine realignment, and the Republican Party is more robust than the Goldwater debacle implied. The torrent of laws rushed through the "fabulous 89th" concealed the fact that many rollcalls turned on a small number of votes; the normal out-party increment in a midterm election may revive conservative authority in the House in 1967.

Above all, the war in Vietnam has complicated predictions. Even more divisive than the Korean conflict, it has raised doubts about Johnson's "credibility"; has blighted the prospects for Administration bills in Congress; has split the Democratic Party; and has tarnished the new image of the Democrats as the party of peace. To finance the war, Johnson has cut back social spending, even on such staples as the school-milk program, and has aborted the war on poverty. The *détente* of Kennedy's last months has given way to a spirit of bellicosity that is inimical to reform. In an article called "The Late, Great Society," the *New Republic* reported that "the war has banked the fires of political innovation throughout government." The Vietnam quandary has resuscitated the Republicans. It has not only increased the likelihood that Goldwater-type candidates will unseat liberal Democrats in November, 1966, thus inaugurating a new period of legislative deadlock, but has even raised the possibility of long-range Republican success. In an era when foreign affairs absorb so much attention, a protracted war may conceivably reshuffle the majority and minority parties, although such an eventuality does not seem imminent.

Even if there is a transformation of national mood, the country will not return to the political universe of the fifties. With the South undergoing rapid change, and the old oligarchs like Harry Byrd gone, the conservative coalition will never have its old potency. After the Supreme Court's reapportionment decisions, rural America will no longer hold the disproportionate power it once exercised. Nor has the full impact of forces like the civil rights movement yet been felt. In the summer of 1965, James Reston wrote: "Maybe at the end of the decade Vietnam will stand out as the historic issue of the Johnson administration, but maybe not. More than likely the transformation of the domestic scene—the acceptance of the New Economics, the redistribution of political power in the South and the cities, the progress in education and social legislation, and the overall movement toward greater discussion between the races and religions and classes—will take on a larger significance than it is given today."

The nationalization of American politics, which accelerated rapidly in the early sixties, seems likely to continue at an even quicker pace in the future. When Vermont votes 67 per cent Democratic and Mississippi 87 per cent Republican, the sectional alignments of the Civil War era have clearly become attentuated. At a time when the parties must adjust to a population explosion which is adding millions of new voters to the electorate, the urbanization of previously single-interest districts is compelling candidates to take stands on national issues in appealing to a more diverse electorate. The epidemic of office-seekers who live outside their constituencies is one more indication of the diminishing importance of locality.

Despite these modifications, the two-party system remains much as it was a century ago. Although political scientists have pressed for greater national party responsibility, and some modest steps have been taken in this direction, the parties remain decentralized institutions. But the durability of the system is impressive. To be sure, it has been argued that voters in the burgeoning suburbs care little about party distinctions, and the remarkable amount of split-ticket voting in 1964 reveals the volatility of party attachment. Yet, for all this, party identification is still the chief determinant of voting, and the two-party system is even expanding its domain. In the South, Negro ballots should speed up the evolution of party competition. Throughout the country, redistricting will open up former sanctuaries of one-party rule. Virtually changeless, the American two-party system has demonstrated repeatedly its adaptability to change.

In the last five years, American political institutions have caught up with most of the pressing problems of the past generation and have begun to face the demands of the last third of this century. The docket of the New Deal has been cleared, and almost everything the Fair Deal stood for has been enacted in some form, from health insurance to civil rights to the Brannan farm plan. More than this, new issues have emerged—demonstration cities, rent supplements, teacher corps; the federal government is concerning itself with topics ranging from birth control to Negro family structure. Our politics still reflects the heritage of both the Civil War and the Great Depression, but today we are in a new time period: 1929 is farther away than the year 2000. In just five years, the country has closed the books on the New Deal legacy and is now looking, for the first time, toward the issues of the twenty-first century.

III

THE LARGE INDUSTRIAL CORPORATION AND THE MAKING OF THE MODERN AMERICAN ECONOMY

by Alfred D. Chandler, Jr.

The previous lectures in this series have reviewed the central developments in two basic modern American institutions—the labor union and the political party. In this third lecture of the series, I plan to examine the history of a second economic institution—the modern corporation. The corporation is, after all, the most important single economic organization in the American economy.[1] Because of its functions and because of the types of decisions made by its managers, I believe that its influence is more pervasive than the labor union, the regulatory commission, or other public bodies concerned with the economy. My focus will be on the most influential and the most complex species of this institutional genus—the integrated and diversified industrial corporation.[2]

[1] The sources of information of this essay come from extended researches, whose findings appear in my "Beginnings of Big Business in American Industry," in *Business History Review,* XXX (Spring, 1959), 1–31; "Development, Diversification and Decentralization," *Postwar Economic Trends in the United States,* ed. Ralph Freeman (Cambridge, 1960), ch. VII; "Le Rôle de la Firme dans l'Économie Américaine," in *Économie Appliquée,* XVII (1964), Nos. 2–3; and *Strategy and Structure: Chapters in the History of the Industrial Enterprise* (Cambridge, Mass., 1962), especially the chapters on Du Pont and General Motors. I am indebted to the Alfred P. Sloan Foundation for support of these studies and of the present one. In the past two years I have been working with Professor Stephen Salsbury on a biography of Pierre S. du Pont, which provides detailed information on the story of that pioneer in modern industrial management.

[2] Included in this definition of the industrial corporation are large marketing enterprises like Sears, Roebuck, Montgomery Ward, General Mills, National Dairy, and others that do their own manufacturing or through their purchasing policies determine the design and price of manufactured articles and so control the flow of goods from the producer of the raw and semi-finished materials to the ultimate consumer.

The large industrial corporation is more varied in its activities and more difficult to manage than are the highly specialized financial, transportation, and public utilities corporations.

Let me begin by reminding you of the dominating position which the giant corporation has acquired in our economy. Consider the statistics on earnings. In 1960 six hundred American corporations had annual earnings of over $10 million. These six hundred represented only 0.5 per cent of the total corporations in the country; yet they accounted for 53 per cent of the total corporate income. Or, if we look only at industrial corporations, in 1960 the four hundred largest of these, all of which had assets of over $100 million, earned 46 per cent of all income earned before taxes in the manufacturing sector and controlled 30 per cent of all assets. Of these the one hundred largest alone accounted for 54 per cent of all profits (not income) in the manufacturing sector.

Consider employment. In 1956 approximately 220 industrials employed more than ten thousand workers. In the aircraft industry 10 such firms employed 94 per cent of the total force; in petroleum 15 such firms employed 86 per cent; in steel 13 firms hired 85 per cent; in motor vehicles 8 firms employed 77 per cent; in office machinery 4 firms employed 71 per cent; in farm machinery 3 put to work 64 per cent; and in electrical machinery 6 employed 50 per cent. Much the same range of figures indicates that in value added, as in employment and income, a few giants handle most of the work in many major American industries. Rather than list more numbers, let me cite just one statistic given in the *New York Times* this fall, for it suggests the size of these giants in relation to other twentieth-century institutions. Last October the *Times* listed the world's largest units according to their gross revenues in the following order: United States, Russia, United Kingdom, France, and then General Motors, followed by West Germany, Japan, and Canada. General Motors' total revenues of just over $20 billion were greater than the combined revenues of Japan and Canada and were very close to United Kingdom's $21 billion and France's $20.5 billion.[3]

[3] *New York Times* (October 31, 1965); and *General Motors Corporation 57th Annual Report, Year Ending December 31, 1965.*

These statistics reflect the critical importance of the decisions made in the general offices of these industrial giants. In a large number of American industries a very small number of men make the final decisions on how much to produce and what prices to charge. Their actions, in turn, intimately affect the economic decisions of hundreds of suppliers, dealers, and retailers, as well as those managers of smaller firms producing or providing comparable or complementary goods for local or specialized markets. This small group also has much to say about employment and wages, although here the decisions are constrained by the desires and opinions of labor union representatives.

The decisions as to output, prices, and wages represent only one type of those made by the managers of large corporations. These and other types are usually tied into two larger and more comprehensive sets of decisions. One of these sets involves the co-ordination of the flow of goods through the various activities of the enterprise, from the production and purchase of the raw and semi-finished materials to the sale to the ultimate consumer. The second and even more critical set involves the allocation of the corporation's resources—money, personnel, and technical and administrative skills. It must be decided how, where, and when the corporation should expand, contract, or stabilize its business and whether it should move in or out of different geographical areas, economic functions, or end products and services. The first set of decisions—those affecting the co-ordination of flow—is determined by short-term estimates of the market and influences the day-to-day pace of the economy. Those involving the allocation of resources are made on the basis of estimates of long-range demand and affect the over-all direction and growth of the national economy.

I plan here to describe the methods and procedures developed over the years by corporation managers in making these two critically important types of decisions. In addition, I plan to indicate how the managers, by using these procedures, help determine the direction of the growth of their corporations, of their industries, and of the economy as a whole. In other words, I will first deal with the developing structure of the modern corporation and then with its changing strategy. But before considering these topics, I must say a little about how and why the large corporations came into being in the first place. This historical background is particularly essential because the institution was *not* created to carry out the critical functions it acquired. Therefore, among the most important tasks which faced the managers of the new institutions were those of devising methods to co-ordinate flow and to allocate resources. Only after these structural devices were completed were the managers able to concentrate on developing new strategies of growth.

The large integrated industrial corporation appeared suddenly and dramatically on the American scene during the last two decades of the nineteenth century. Before that time decisions affecting the flow of goods through the economy and the allocations of its resources were extremely decentralized. They were made in hundreds of thousands of small family firms. These firms normally handled a single product or function. The business decisions of their owners were normally affected by an impersonal market over which they had relatively little control, except possibly in nearby local areas. Price determined the volume of output and also the pace of the flow of goods from the producer of raw materials to the factory and then to the ultimate consumer via an intricate network of wholesalers.

The great transformation from decentralized decision-making to centralized co-ordination and control of production and distribution came at the very end of the last century. Between 1897 and 1902 there occurred the first and still the most significant merger movement in American history. In industry after industry the giant enterprise appeared. The merger movement which marked the beginning of the modern structure of American business was itself the culmination of a creative period of industrial and corporate growth.

The modern corporation had its beginnings in the eighteen fifties with the swift spread of the railroad network and the factory system during that decade. The railroads, as the nation's first big business, came to provide the only available model for financing and administering the giant industrial enterprises. The railroads played this role because their promoters, financers, and managers were the first to build, finance, and operate business enterprises requiring massive capital investment and calling for complex administrative arrangements. The financing of the railroads required such large amounts of money that it brought into being modern Wall Street and its specialized investment bankers. The instruments and methods later used to capitalize large industrial enterprises were all employed earlier by the railroads, for financial requirements forced the use of the corporate form. An individual or partnership simply could not supply enough capital to build even a small railroad. The sale of corporate stocks and bonds was essential. The modern holding company, too, had its start in the railroads, for the management of interstate business encouraged one railroad corporation to control others in other states by purchasing and holding their stock.

The railroads were forced to pioneer in modern business administration as well as in modern corporate finance. Their managers fashioned large functional departments to handle transportation, traffic, and finance. They set up central offices to supervise and co-ordinate the work of the departments and the railroads as a whole. They originated line and staff distinctions in business organization. They were the first to develop a flow of operating statistics used to control movement of traffic and also to evaluate the performance of operating departments. They also had to meet brand-new problems of modern cost accounting, to make the distinctions between variable, constant, and joint costs, to differentiate between working and fixed capital, and to account for depreciation and even obsolescence.

But the railroad was only the model. The parent of the large corporation was the factory. The modern factory with its power-driven machinery and its permanent working force, whose tasks were subdivided and specialized, appeared in the United States as early as 1814. Yet until the swift spread of an all-weather transportation network, including the railroad, the ocean-going steamship, and the telegraph, relatively few factories existed in the United States outside of the textile and related industries. Then in the late eighteen forties and fifties factory production began for the first time to be significant in the making of sewing machines, clocks, watches, ploughs, reapers, shoes, suits and other ready-made clothing, and rifles and pistols for commercial use. The same years saw the spread of the large integrated iron works, using coal and coke instead of charcoal for fuel. The Civil War further stimulated the growth in these industries. After the war the factory spread to others. By 1880 the census reported that of the three million people employed in industries using machines, four fifths worked under the factory system of production. "Remarkable applications of this system," the census added, "are to be found in the manufacture of boots, shoes, watches, musical instruments, clothing, metal goods, general firearms, carriages and wagons, woolen goods, rubber goods, and even the slaughtering of hogs."[4]

In the quarter of a century following the completion of this census, the factory was transformed in many industries into a vertically integrated, multifunctional enterprise. Let me explain what I mean by these terms. In 1880 nearly all manufacturing firms only manufactured. The factory owners purchased their raw materials and sold their finished goods through wholesalers, who were sometimes commission agents and at other times jobbers who took title to the goods. By the first years of the twentieth century, however, many American industries were dominated by enterprises that had created their own distributing organizations, sometimes including even retailing outlets, and had formed their own purchasing systems, in some cases controlling their supplies of semi-finished and raw materials.

Many reasons have been suggested for this fundamental change. These include the impact of new technology, the influence of shifting overseas demand for American goods, the development of the market for industrial securities, the

[4] Carroll D. Wright, "The Factory System of the United States," in U.S. Census Office, *Report on the Manufactures of the United States at the 10th Census, June 1, 1880* (Washington, D.C., 1883), p. 548.

desire for tighter market control, the tariff, and even the sinister motives of those energetic and somewhat romantic fellows, the Robber Barons.[5] I would like to propose two other more specific and, I believe, more significant reasons for the growth of the large integrated enterprise. One was the inability of factory owners to enforce and so maintain cartels. If the American cartels had had some kind of legal support or had been sanctioned by the government as was often true in Europe, the giant corporation would have been slower in developing. The other reason was the inadequacy of the existing wholesaler network to handle high volume distribution of goods.

The manufacturers who pioneered in building the integrated firm were those who first found the wholesaler network inadequate for their needs. They were of two types. First, there were the volume producers of durable goods, who discovered that the wholesaler was unable to handle the initial demonstration to customers, unable to provide the necessary consumer credit, and unable to ensure continuing repair and service of goods sold. Second, there were the producers of perishable goods for the mass market, and they found the wholesaler still more inadequate. Among the first type were the makers of sewing machines, agricultural implements, typewriters, cash registers, carriages, bicycles, and, most important of all, electrical machinery and equipment. The McCormicks in reapers, the Remingtons in typewriters, Edward Clark of Singer Sewing Machine, James Patterson in cash registers, Albert Pope in bicycles, William C. Durant in carriages, and George Westinghouse and Charles Coffin in electrical machinery all pioneered in the creation of national and even international marketing organizations. Their new

[5] These views are well summarized in Ralph Andreano's comments on studies by Ralph Nelson and others in his *New Views on American Economic Development* (Cambridge, 1966), pp. 15–19. A recent study that gives further evidence of the inability of the pools to maintain price and production schedules is Peter Temin, *Iron and Steel in Nineteenth Century America—An Economic Inquiry* (Cambridge, 1965), pp. 175–89. Of all the products in the iron and steel industry the only effective pool for any amount of time was in rails, and even here it was successful for only short periods.

distributing networks usually included franchised retail dealers supported by branch offices which supplied the retailers with a flow of products, funds, spare parts and accessories, and with specialized repair and maintenance men. In order to assure supplies for the large volume of production needed to meet the demands of the new distributing system, these innovators also built large purchasing organizations, often bought or erected factories to manufacture parts and semi-finished materials, and sometimes came to own their own large tracts of lumber or iron and steel works.

In these same years, the eighties and nineties, the volume producers of perishable goods for the mass market created their own distributing and purchasing organizations. Among these Gustavus Swift, a New England wholesale butcher, was probably the most significant innovator. In the late seventies Swift appreciated, as had others, that the urbanizing East was outrunning its meat supply. Swift also saw the possibilities, which only a few others appreciated, of using the refrigerated car to bring western meat to the East. The shipment of live cattle east, which since the eighteen fifties had been the most lucrative eastbound trade for the railroads, was inefficient and costly. Sixty per cent of the animal was inedible. Cattle lost weight or died on the trip. What was equally important, concentration of butchering in Chicago would assure high volume operations and a much lower unit cost than the current method of shipping in small lots to wholesale butchers throughout the East.

Gustavus Swift's basic innovation was the creation of a distribution network. He realized that the refrigerated car was not enough. Carloads of fresh meat could hardly be dumped in Baltimore or Boston on a hot summer's day. So in the eighties he began to build branch houses in every major town or city in the East and in many other parts of the nation. A branch house included a refrigerated warehouse, a sales office, and men and equipment to deliver meat to retail butchers and food stores. In carrying out this plan, Swift met the most determined opposition. The railroads were startled by the prospect of losing a major business, so the Eastern Truck Line Association refused to carry his refrigerated cars. In 1886 the wholesalers organized the Butchers National Protection Association to fight the "trust."

But good meat at low price won out. Once the market was assured, Swift then set up large packing houses in the cities along the cattle frontier and even bought into the stockyards. By the end of the eighties wholesalers with ample energy and resources realized that unless they quickly followed Swift's example they would have to remain small local enterprises. Armour, Cudahy, Hammond, Morris, and the firm of Schwartzchild and Sulzberger (it became Wilson and Company in World War I) quickly built their branch networks and bought into stockyards. These remained the "big six" in the meat-packing industry until changes in transportation and refrigeration in the nineteen thirties and forties opened new opportunities.

What Swift did for meat, Andrew Preston did in the same years for the mass distribution of bananas through the creation of the United Fruit Company. Also in the eighties large brewers like Schlitz, Blatz, and Pabst in Milwaukee and Anheuser-Busch in St. Louis set up comparable distribution networks based on refrigeration. In the same decade James B. Duke did the same thing for a new non-refrigerated product—the cigarette.

These pioneers in high volume manufacturing and distribution of both perishable and relatively complex durable goods demonstrated the clear economies of scale. They provided obvious models for manufacturers who had until then found the existing wholesaler network quite satisfactory. Nevertheless, the factory owners in these industries were slow to follow the example of Swift, McCormick, and the others. They had to be pushed rather than attracted into adopting a strategy of vertical integration and with it the economies of mass production and mass distribution. It was the continuing oppressive pressure of falling prices between the mid-eighties and the mid-nineties that provided this push and forced many manufacturers to organize for the mass national market. The price decline, in turn, may have resulted largely from the coming of the factory itself. Far more efficient than hand or shop production, the widespread adoption of the factory after 1850, and particularly after the Civil War, had led to a sharply increasing output of goods and an excess of supply over demand.

In many American industries these falling prices resulted in a similar organizational response. The pattern was the same in producers' goods industries like iron, steel, brass, copper, rubber products, and explosives, and in consumers' goods industries like salt, sugar, matches, biscuits, kerosene, and rubber boots and shoes. This pattern—the second route to great size—was one of combination, consolidation, and then vertical integration. To meet the threat of falling prices and profits, the factory owners formed trade associations whose primary function was to control price and production. But these associations were rarely able to maintain their cartels. If the prices became stabilized, some manufacturers would leave the association and obtain business by selling below the established price. If prices rose temporarily, the members often disbanded until the downward trend began again. The associations proved to be, in the words of the first president of the Petroleum Refiners' Association, John D. Rockefeller, "ropes of sand." They failed for the same reason as did the railroad cartels in the seventies and eighties. The agreements could not be enforced. They did not have the binding effect of a legal contract.

While the railroad men turned unsuccessfully to advocating pooling legalized by state and national legislatures, the manufacturers devised new ways of acquiring firmer legal control of the factories in their industries. Initially they began to purchase stock in competing companies. Then came a new device, the trust. The stocks of the various manufacturing companies were turned over to a board of trustees, with the owners of the stock receiving trust certificates in return. Less cumbersome was the holding company, whose stock could be exchanged directly for that of an operating firm and could then be bought or sold in the security markets. Once New Jersey had passed a general incorporation law for holding companies in 1889, this instrument became the standard one by which a group of manufacturers obtained legal control over a large number of factories.

Administrative control and industrial reorganization often, though not always, followed legal consolidation. The factories controlled by the trust or the holding company were placed under a single manager with a specialized staff. The manager closed down the smaller, more inefficient plants and enlarged the more efficient ones. By running a much smaller number of much larger plants day and night, he quickly lowered unit costs. As a high volume producer, the consolidated enterprise now found it could no longer rely on the fragmented distributing network of wholesalers. The enterprise therefore quickly moved into setting up its own wholesalers and occasionally even its own retailers and its own purchasing organization, often moving back to control of raw material.

The petroleum industry was one of the very first to combine, then to consolidate legally and administratively, and then to integrate, because it was one of the very first to overproduce for the national and international markets. In the early seventies both refiners and producers of petroleum formed trade associations to control price and production. They were completely unsuccessful in enforcing their rulings throughout the industry. So in the mid-seventies Rockefeller, by using railroad rates as a weapon, was able to bring a large portion of the refiners under the legal control of his Standard Oil Company.

However, legal control proved to be insufficient. Standard's primary market was abroad (for in the eighteen seventies close to 90 per cent of refined petroleum went to Europe). Rockefeller therefore had to develop an efficient operating organization at home if he was to compete successfully abroad. So his company tightened up its legal control through the formation of the first modern business trust. Then between 1883 and 1885 the refineries were consolidated. Where the Standard Oil Trusts had operated fifty-five plants in 1882, it had only twenty-two in 1886. Three fourths of all its production was concentrated in three giant refineries. As a result, unit costs dropped dramatically. By 1884 Standard's average cost of refining a barrel of oil was already 0.534 cents, as compared to 1.5 cents in the rest of the industry.[6] The trust then began to set up its own extensive distributing network, and in the late eighties it started to integrate backwards, going for the first time into the production of crude; that is, taking the crude oil out of the ground.

In the late eighteen eighties and early nineties manufacturers in other industries began to follow the example of Standard Oil, Swift, and McCormick. The severe depression of the mid-nineties slowed the processes. Funds to finance the new holding companies, to help them tempt other manufacturers into the consolidation, to pay for the necessary reorganization of production and distribution facilities, and to finance the purchase or construction of plants and mines producing raw or semi-finished materials were hard to find. Indeed, some of the newly formed consolidations failed to survive the depression. Then as prosperity returned in 1897 and capital became easier to obtain, industry after industry came to be dominated by a handful of large integrated corporations.[7] The promise of handsome returns from high volume production and high volume distribution and the harsh memory of twenty years of falling prices made the prospect of consolidation and integration difficult to resist. The result was the first great merger movement in American history.

In the years immediately following this merger movement, one of the greatest challenges facing the managers of the newly integrated corporation was to develop procedures to assure their efficient operation. This was no easy task, for many of the factory managers had long been competitors,

[6] Harold F. Williamson and Arnold R. Daum, *The American Petroleum Industry, The Age of Illumination, 1859–1899* (Evanston, Ill., 1959), pp. 475, 483–84.

[7] Hans B. Thorelli, *Federal Anti-Trust Policy* (Baltimore, 1957), pp. 275, 294–303, provides tables and lists of those companies formed before and after the depression of the nineties. Significantly, in industries where the wholesale network was deeply entrenched and had its own trade associations, such as in hardware, lumber, coal, furniture, textiles, and ready-made clothing industries, there was some consolidation but much less than in other industries.

often bitter rivals. The wholesalers now transformed into sales executives had had in the past different interests and attitudes from those of the manufacturers. So too had the purchasing agents. Moreover, these men, long used to operating independently, did not take kindly either to personal or to accounting or statistical controls.

To unite these men and offices into a smooth working organization involved two basic tasks, the building of new functional departments and the creation of a central office. The formation of the functional departments often called for massive reorganization of an industry's production, distribution, and purchasing facilities. The setting up of the central office required the development of procedures to assure a steady and regular flow of goods and materials through the several departments in the interest of the corporation as a whole.

Some managers of the new integrated enterprises, like those of General Electric, International Harvester, Bethlehem Steel, and Du Pont, began almost immediately to work out their administrative structures. Others, like those of Allis-Chalmers, Westinghouse, and United States Steel, moved more slowly, often acting only when forced by declining profits and financial difficulties. Let me indicate the administrative challenges facing these corporations and the nature of their responses by reviewing briefly the experience of one of the more energetic and imaginative pioneers in organization building, the E. I. du Pont de Nemours Powder Company.

In 1902 three young cousins—Coleman, Alfred, and Pierre du Pont—took over control of their family firm, then just a century old. They immediately arranged to consolidate with their largest and normally friendly rival, Laflin & Rand. Next they brought smaller firms into the consolidation by forming a holding company, the E. I. du Pont de Nemours Powder Company, and then exchanging its stock for that of the smaller companies who were members of the old Gunpowder Trade Association. Next they disbanded this trade association, which had been attempting to set price and production schedules fairly regularly since 1873 (and had been able to do so only because its leading members, Du Pont and Laflin & Rand, purchased stock of other members).

Department building quickly followed legal consolidation. The holding company became an operating one. The many factories were placed under one of three operating departments—black powder, high explosives (that is, dynamite), and smokeless powder. Branch sales offices were created in all parts of the country and placed under a central sales department. An essential materials department was formed to handle the new high volume purchasing of nitrates, glycerine, sulphur, and pyrites, for with consolidation the company had become the largest single purchaser in the United States of these materials. In fact, after 1902 the Du Pont Company alone accounted for 5 per cent of the world consumption and 30 per cent of the United States consumption of nitrate, and one sixth of the world and one third of the United States consumption of glycerine.[8]

The Du Pont cousins fashioned staff as well as line departments. The new development department concentrated on investigating and planning possibilities for capital expenditures and, until the formation of the chemical department, administered the research laboratories set up to improve the product. The engineering department specialized in plant and office construction and maintenance. The traffic department helped assure an efficient flow of materials from the nitrate beds of Chile to the mining and construction companies who used the finished explosives. In addition, there was a legal department and one for personnel. Finally, there was the treasury department, which had both line and staff duties. Besides taking on the routine work of handling funds coming in and out of the company, it paid close attention to improving cost and accounting figures needed by the central office to carry on the administration of the company as a whole.

The process of department building required many persons in the new company to adopt new roles, new values,

[8] These figures come from internal reports of the Du Pont Company. They and their implications will be given in more detail in the forthcoming biography of Pierre S. du Pont.

and new modes of action. In the case of Du Pont, the salesmen resisted the new ways more vehemently than did the factory managers. One highly respected agent considered the home office's request for systematic accounting information a direct slap at his business honor and soon retired in a huff. Another found reporting regularly to Wilmington so inhibiting to his taste that he left the company, taking with him all the records of the Gunpowder Trade Association (the old cartel), which he later used to bring an antitrust suit against Du Pont. Most of the men involved did not react so strongly, but in personal terms the transition from combination to consolidation and integration was by no means easy.

At the same time a central office had to be fashioned to administer the work of the departments. At Du Pont, as in most of the new giants, the company's ruling body was the executive committee, composed of the president and heads of the major departments. The committee considered its task one of appraising the performance and co-ordination of the work of the several departments and planning for the future growth of the company as a whole. And it was in carrying out these tasks that the committee became quickly involved in devising ways to co-ordinate flows and allocate resources.

The methods involved in the allocation of resources were the easiest to devise. First came procedures to provide information about each of the many requests for capital expenditures sent by the departments to the executive committee. Besides detailed data on costs, the committee asked for anticipated rate of return from the expenditure and estimates on how much the new construction or equipment would reduce current operating costs. In addition, each appropriation request had to be checked and approved by staff specialists in the engineering, traffic, and purchasing departments to see that all possible savings were achieved and specialized problems worked out.

The committee was soon getting the information it wanted, but the difficulty was that its members did not have time to digest it. So they delegated to plant managers and department heads the authorization of smaller capital expenditures. They appointed one full-time senior executive and his office staff to review appropriation requests and check on their execution. Finally, before the end of 1905, the committee decided to devote alternate weekly meetings to deciding on appropriations. This new emphasis of the powder-making industry's top decision-making body provides a striking demonstration of the functional differences between the old combination or cartel and the new consolidated, integrated enterprise. In 1902 the central committee of the Gunpowder Trade Association still met weekly. It discussed only specific adjustments of price and never considered the allocation of resources. In 1905 the executive committee of the new Powder Company was already concentrating over half its time on the allocation of resources. It rarely discussed prices, and then only in terms of general policy.[9] The specifics of pricing were left wholly to the sales department.

The next step in systematizing appropriation procedures was to tie the many departmental requests into a broad plan for company growth. This led to having each department submit annual estimates for capital expenditures as well as for their operating needs. On the basis of these estimates from the departments, the treasurer's financial forecasts, and a flow of information from the staff departments, particularly the development department, the executive committee made its decisions among the many claims of the several operating departments. To guide its decisions, the members began, after 1905, to work out a flexible long-term plan of growth based on extended long-range estimates of market demand.

The development of methods and techniques to co-ordinate flow of materials through the enterprise raised more critical challenges to the managers of Du Pont and other new giants than did the formulation of appropriation procedures. Such co-ordination of mass production and mass distribution involved several quite different but closely re-

[9] For example, the executive committee agreed in 1905 on a pricing policy for black powder which would net the company a profit of fifteen cents a barrel and which would permit the most efficient small competitors five cents a barrel and the less efficient still less.

lated matters, including the handling and adjusting of the fluctuating demands of working capital, the control of inventory at all stages of the flow, the physical movements of goods and materials from the sources of raw materials to the ultimate consumer, and finally the improvement and alteration of the quality and design of the product to meet the customers' changing needs and demands. All but the last of these problems became less difficult when supply or output was closely related to demand.[10] If materials could flow smoothly through the enterprise from the purchase of raw materials to the final sale of the product, working capital requirements could be reduced, inventories of raw materials and semi-finished goods could be kept at a minimum, retailers and customers could be assured of a steady and more certain supply, and employment could become more stable. Moreover, because a steady flow would permit the efficient use of all the company's facilities, it would help lower unit costs. To assure such a flow, an effective traffic department, concerned only with the physical flow of goods, was important but hardly in itself enough.

The problem of co-ordinating a massive flow of materials through all phases of an industry's activities was of course a brand-new one. Until the coming of the integrated firm there was no such central co-ordinating agency in any American industry. This function was not, as I have stressed, ever developed by the cartels or trade associations. Before the formation of the integrated firm, goods moved slowly in small lots from mine or farm to factory and then to customer through the extended wholesaler network. Each step normally involved a separate financial transaction and a delay in the wholesaler's warehouse or store. Three or four months from mine to factory and again from factory to customer was quite normal. During that period of time, demand for the finished goods and availability of raw and semi-finished materials often changed.

[10] To assure a liaison between the sales, operating, and development departments so that the products would be altered to meet customer needs and competitive developments, the Du Pont executive committee followed the example of the large electric and steel companies in forming a consumers' service office.

The meat packers, who created some of the very first of the integrated enterprises, were quickly able to assure an almost instantaneous connection between supply and demand. The branch houses telegraphed their orders daily to the packing plants. All messages were cleared through Chicago, where a complete record of all plants and yards was maintained. When one plant could not fill an order completely, the Chicago office would have the remainder supplied by another plant which had reported a surplus. The packing plants in turn had direct contact with the stockyards. So even as the cattle moved onto the disassembling line, the final destination of the many parts and accessories was already known.

Such co-ordination of flow of perishable refrigerated products was relatively simple. Other new enterprises had to obtain a variety of raw materials and other supplies from a great distance, often from overseas. They produced a greater number of products in widely scattered plants and marketed their line through an even more widespread distribution network. For these companies instantaneous communication linking supply and demand was not enough. Purchasing and production had to be based not on present but on future demand. An accurate forecast of the market had become essential.

For the makers of producers' goods, like the Du Ponts, forecasting was not too difficult. The number of customers was less than in consumers' goods industries and their needs easier to anticipate. Before World War I the Du Pont departments concerned—sales, operating, and purchasing—made their own separate forecasts based on careful consultation with one another. Immediately after World War I, however, when the Du Pont Company began to diversify into other lines, particularly into consumers' goods like paints and varnishes, these relatively informal arrangements broke down. The sharp postwar recession caught the Du Pont Company, as it did so many other large industrials, with a huge surplus of supplies of finished and unfinished materials. This depression, in fact, created the first modern inventory crisis in American industry, because it was the first really severe depression to occur since the coming of the integrated enterprise at the turn of the century. The overstocking of inventory and the resulting large losses brought a major administrative reorganization at Du Pont and other corporations.

For the volume producers of consumer durables the forecast of demand was even more critical than it was to those making producers' goods. This was particularly true of those firms whose products were relatively high-priced durables which involved a great number of materials, parts, and accessories in their production, as did, for example, household appliances and automobiles. It is hardly surprising, therefore, that the young, expanding automobile industry suffered a more serious inventory and accompanying financial crisis in 1921 than any other American business. Henry Ford rode out the storm by forcing his cars on his dealers, thereby making the local agents and their banks provide the necessary capital to carry the inventory. General Motors, with less market power and less executive nerve, had to write off $82 million worth of inventories as a dead loss.

Because of the heavy investment the Du Pont Company had made in General Motors, the Du Ponts then took over its management. The new president, Pierre du Pont, considered his first task as one of administrative reorganization. After defining the boundaries of the operating divisions and the new general office, he and his associates put into effect the appropriation procedures they had already developed in Wilmington. They also began to apply the Du Pont experience in co-ordinating the flow of goods through the enterprises to the more complex situation in the automobile industry.

By 1925 the General Motors managers had tied all the factors involved in mass production and mass distribution to an annual forecast of demand. These forecasts were employed to allocate working capital and to control inventory, production, employment and car delivery schedules, and the executive committee also used them to determine costs and prices, to appraise divisional performance, and to assist in the allocation of basic resources. This is the way the new forecasting procedures worked. Each year, every division regularly compiled a "divisional index" for the approval of the executive committee. It was based on long-term estimates of national growth, seasonal variations in demand, business fluctuations, and anticipated share of the market. These indices were constantly adjusted as ten-day reports from dealers and monthly reports of new car registrations indicated the precise nature of consumer demand.[11] On the first day of each month the estimates of output, inventory, purchases, etc., were made definite for the next month and made more exact for the following three months. The approval of the monthly schedule thus provided authorization for the following month's purchases. "The usual practice," reported one General Motors executive in 1926, "is to release immediately upon adoption of the schedule the materials required for the following month, and to make definite commitments beyond that time, that is, one month, only for those items which require a longer period for their manufacture and delivery to the plant."[12]

In addition, the annual divisional indices provided detailed estimates on cost, prices, and profits, which the executive committee used in allocating the company's resources. Because unit costs varied so directly with volume in this largest of all mass production industries, costs came to be based on standard volume of 80 per cent of capacity. But satisfactory cost data could only be acquired after Pierre du Pont had instituted a uniform and detailed system of cost accounting throughout the entire huge corporation. On the basis of uniform costs and of both standard and estimated volume, the executive committee approved prices recommended by the division. On the basis of the resulting profit margins and volume of sales, the committee evaluated the performance of the divisions. Finally, by using these

[11] The monthly reports of new car registration were supplied by the R. L. Polk Company, which, by showing the exact figures on all new cars registered, gave the executive committee constant information on each division's share of the market.

[12] Albert Bradley, "Setting Up a Forecasting Program," *Annual Convention Series, American Management Association,* No. 41 (March, 1926), reprinted in Alfred D. Chandler, Jr. (ed.), *Giant Enterprise* (New York, 1964), p. 136.

evaluations, the divisional forecasts, and staff-prepared long-term estimates of the market and the economy, the committee allocated the resources it controlled by reviewing, reworking, and approving capital and operating budgets and by promoting and transferring top operating personnel.

During the nineteen twenties similar complex techniques were worked out and adopted by other giant enterprises for controlling flows and allocating resources. The recession of 1921 provided the initial impetus to a number of large corporations other than Du Pont and General Motors.[13] General Motors executives themselves encouraged the spread of these methods by describing their achievements at professional meetings and in professional journals. In the mid-twenties the large oil firms, which had not been so hard hit by the 1921 recession, started to work out details of such procedures as they began to be caught in a squeeze resulting from a leveling off of demand for gasoline at the very moment when the opening of the mid-continent fields greatly increased supply. Standard Oil was the first, when it set up its co-ordination and budgeting departments in 1925. Others soon followed its example. After 1929 the coming of the great depression hastened the adoption of these new cost-cutting procedures in this and other industries.

In the thirties and forties these and other corporate techniques even spread to the public sector of the economy. As national income contracted after the 1929 stock market crash, those corporations which had adopted the new co-ordinating procedures were able to roll with the punch. (For example, in 1931 General Motors still made a profit of $117 million, while Henry Ford, who never had any use for these bureaucratic methods, lost $32 million.) But even these enterprises could do little to retard the economy's headlong decline. Only the government was in a position to take strong positive action. As it began to play a larger role in the economy, government officials increasingly made use of the legal and administrative advantages of the cor-

[13] *Strategy and Structure,* pp. 231–32, suggests the impact of the recession on the development of inventory and other controls at Sears, Roebuck.

poration. Where in 1932 there had been less than a dozen government corporations, there were ninety by 1937 and just over one hundred at the end of World War II.[14] While a majority of these were financial corporations, a good number did handle the production and distribution of goods and quickly adopted the procedures developed earlier by the private corporations.

World War II encouraged in other ways the spread of these procedures in both the private and public sectors of the economy. One was through government contracts for war production. The system of payment under these contracts required a multitude of businesses, particularly relatively small ones, to adopt for the first time effective cost accounting methods, which are the essential basis of all statistical controls. Far more important was the fact that by late 1942 the war economy came to be managed by means of the business forecast. In 1942, when war needs replaced consumer markets as the determinant of end products, the War Production Board attempted to allocate scarce materials by the use of priorities. Priorities, however, did not work at all. The basic difficulty was that the Board issued priorities on materials and components that did not yet exist. Such priorities became only hunting licenses. In the complex production of durable goods, as industrialists had earlier discovered, supply simply could not respond that quickly to demand, even to demand created by government fiat. A lead time was necessary.

The solution to these difficulties was suggested in the summer of 1942 by Ferdinand Eberstadt, an investment banker who was in charge of naval procurement. He proposed what became known as the Controlled Materials Plan, which tied the allocation of critically scarce metals like iron, steel, copper, and aluminum, and, a little later, of components like motors, generators, and compressors, into the forecasting procedures developed by General Motors and

[14] The growth and uses of the corporation in the federal government is summarized in John C. James, "A Report on Public Corporations in the Federal Government," an unpublished study prepared in the summer of 1965 at the Center for the Study of Recent American History at The Johns Hopkins University.

other large corporations.[15] By this plan, the makers of the few most critical materials and components forwarded to the War Production Board forecasts of their output for the next three months. At the same time, the major claimant agencies—the Army, Navy, Shipping Board, Lend-Lease, synthetic rubber, and high-octane gasoline programs—sent the Board three-month estimates of their needs. The Requirements Committee of the War Production Board then worked out allocations of the output of the critical items, notifying the claimant agencies of their quotas two months in advance of actual production. The agencies then allocated their quotas among the prime contractors, who received them one month in advance of production. These prime contractors, usually the large corporations, then adjusted their production schedules and those of most of their subcontractors and suppliers in accordance with their allocation. Thus, when the basic materials were produced, they went directly to the prime and subcontractors for immediate use.

As Eberstadt explained when he proposed his plan to the W.P.B.: "The above system has the merit of confining decisions at the highest levels to broad questions and decentralizing the detail. . . . The basic distribution of materials between the military, basic economic, Lend-Lease, and other exports would be made by the War Production Board . . . but the actual scheduling and directing of materials, particularly in the military field, would be taken over by those responsible for procurement and production, which cannot be carried out without control of the flow of materials in accordance with their schedules."[16] In nearly all cases the large corporations continued to co-ordinate the flow from the initial supplier to the claimant agency. But where production had not yet come under the large corporation, as in the case of landing craft, the responsible agency, in this

[15] The story of the formation, adoption, and operation of the Controlled Material Plan and its counterpart, the Component Schedule Plan, is well told in J. Elberton Smith, *The Army and Economic Mobilization* (Washington, D.C., 1959), ch. XXV, pp. 597–99.

[16] *Ibid.*, pp. 567–70.

case the Navy, had to work out the co-ordination of flows at the cost of a great deal of time and energy.

In this way, then, the war helped to make the forecast, like modern cost accounting, a standard operating procedure for much of American industry. The success of the Controlled Materials Plan and the Component Scheduling Plan, particularly when compared to the earlier chaos in war production, emphasized the key role the large corporation had played in co-ordinating the flow of materials through the American economy. Their successes also suggest the value of the procedures which the corporation managers had developed for the management of a command as well as a market economy.

With the return of peace the War Production Board was disbanded, and market demand again became the basic criterion for decisions concerning the allocation of resources and the co-ordination of flows. And these critical economic decisions remained concentrated, as they had been since 1900, in the hands of corporation managers. As the procedures for co-ordinating flows became increasingly systematized and routinized, the senior executives of these large corporations were able to concentrate more and more on the most significant of their functions, the allocation of the resources under their control. I want now to consider briefly how the managers used their long- and short-term forecasts and their appropriation procedures to allocate funds, personnel, and technical and managerial know-how. In particular, I want to examine the underlying business strategies which the managers used as criteria for allocating their resources. I want also to explain why the managers shifted from one basic strategy, that of vertical integration, to another, that of diversification.

During the first two decades of the twentieth century, the men in charge of the large corporations continued to follow the strategy of vertical integration, which had been so critical to the formation of their corporations. This strategy particularly continued to dominate the new industries, such as automobiles and chemicals, which only began to move into high volume production and distribution in these decades. The strategy was also significant to companies in industries like petroleum and rubber, which were transformed by the coming of the automobile. But even the corporations that had come into being during the great merger movement at the turn of the century at first continued to grow largely by integrating backwards.

The reasons for specific moves varied. Rate of return on investment was a critical criterion. Often, however, the move to purchase or build a factory making semi-finished materials or a mine producing raw materials was made for defensive reasons. The need to assure the steady flow of raw and semi-finished materials at a reasonable price led to the buying or building of facilities at below the normal expected rate of return. This was true when the Du Ponts moved into the manufacture of glycerine and fusel oil and when the United States Rubber Company purchased rubber plantations in Sumatra. Sometimes the mere threat of backward integration was enough to assure materials from suppliers on reasonable schedules and at reasonable prices. General Motors, for example, used this threat successfully in obtaining its tires, as did Du Pont in getting its supplies of sulphuric and nitric acid. Companies often found the production of raw or semi-finished materials quite profitable, as did Du Pont in its Chilean nitrate production, Jersey Standard and Socony in the production of crude oil, and General Motors in its parts and accessory business. If this were so, their managers would allocate further resources to these areas even before they would expand their more traditional manufacturing and distributing activities.

Very few corporations, however, advocated complete and total integration—that is, the ownership and control of all activities involved in the production and distribution of their products. The General Motors executives emphatically opposed Henry Ford's example of building one massive manufacturing plant to produce a single model and of owning the sources of nearly all the supplies that went into its production. They believed that the forecasting and other procedures they were developing were as efficient in assuring a steady volume of production, as well as being far more flexible in meeting changing market demands, than were Ford's technological achievements in physical co-ordination. In fact, the effective control of their integrated operation by statistical means helped make General Motors one of the most profitable in the nation after 1925, while Ford's attempt at physical rather than statistical co-ordination was one basic reason for his astonishingly poor profit performance in the same years.

When the nation's economy began to level off in the twenties and when it stumbled badly in the thirties, firms in the more technologically advanced industries began to shift from a strategy of integration to one of diversification; that is, they began to allocate resources for the development of new products for new kinds of markets. Those that took up the new strategy did so precisely because the leveling and then the decline in demand left their managers faced with the threat of a decreasing rate of return from their resources. Companies whose resources were most easily transferable to the production and distribution of new products were the first to diversify. A few firms with a large investment in research and development started on the new strategy in the twenties. Those with resources concentrated in distribution facilities began hesitantly to follow suit in the thirties, while those whose primary investment was in production facilities made few attempts to diversify, even after World War II.

In 1938 five industries employed three fourths of all persons working in organized American industrial research. They were the chemical, electrical, rubber, petroleum, and power machinery industries. (The last group included automobile and agricultural machinery companies.) In the twenties chemical and electrical companies began to develop new end products for markets quite different from those of their traditional lines. The Du Pont Company pioneered by turning its skills and organization developed in nitrocellulose technology into the mass production and distribution of paints, artificial leather, films, synthetic fibers, dyestuffs, and heavy chemicals. Later in the twenties Hercules developed several lines of products on a naval stores base. Dow soon began to diversify on the basis of salt chemistry, while Monsanto did the same on sugar. Union Carbide in its early diversification relied on calcium carbide, and Tennessee Eastman on cellulose acetate.

The story of the electrical industry is comparable. Until the twenties General Electric and Westinghouse had concentrated almost wholly on the development, manufacturing, and marketing of electric power and light. Then after World War I they began to develop household appliances such as stoves, washing machines, heaters, vacuum cleaners, and refrigerators. The explicit reason given for the move was that appliances would use excess capacity in the small motor and other divisions and at the same time increase the demand for power-generating equipment. In addition, the research laboratories turned out a number of new products such as radio tubes, X-rays, and alloys. Where, on the basis of rate of return on investment, the new product could make use of some existing facilities and personnel, the company took on its manufacture and distribution. If it could not, then it licensed the product to be manufactured elsewhere.

The continuing rapid growth of automobile production up to 1925 delayed diversification in the petroleum and rubber industries. However, the two large rubber firms, United States Rubber and Goodrich, which were formed before the development of the tire did begin to diversify after World War I. So too did the large power machinery makers who were not involved in producing passenger cars, such as International Harvester and Allis-Chalmers. With the beginning of the depression, however, the automobile and allied industries began to diversify. The tire companies started to develop products based on rubber chemistry. General Motors moved into airplanes, aircraft engines, and diesels. In the latter case, it revolutionized the American locomotive industry. The petroleum companies moved more slowly than the other two industries, but by the end of the thirties two or three companies were producing petrochemicals. In the thirties, too, General Foods, General Mills, and Borden's (milk) began to use their marketing organizations to sell a number of new products. So did International Paper, American Can, and Pittsburgh Plate Glass. These last three had a heavier investment in distribution than in production facilities.

The war had a far greater impact than the depression on bringing on diversification, and for very different reasons. The war permitted companies in a wide range of industries to amass resources used for the manufacture of products quite different from their traditional lines. For example, the huge synthetic rubber program fully committed rubber and petroleum corporations to the production of chemicals. After the war, nearly all the major oil and rubber companies began producing petrochemicals, rubber chemicals, plastics, and many sorts of synthetics; and the automobile companies began turning out tractors, farm equipment, marine engines, and other non-automotive products. At the same time the war-stimulated electronics revolution had opened new fields for General Electric, Westinghouse, and the smaller electrical manufacturers in television, computers, and transistors.

Corporation managers soon discovered that the new strategy required a new administrative structure. The first to devise it were those rational executives in charge of the Du Pont Company, one of the very first companies to diversify. The basic reason for the reorganization was that the move from operating in one industry to operating in many industries sharply increased both the short-range and long-term decisions made at the central office, and particularly those concerned with the co-ordination of flows and the allocation of resources. The Du Pont executives therefore created a new structure consisting of autonomous, integrated product divisions and a general office consisting of general and staff executives concerned with the operations of the corporation as a whole. The primary task of the division managers was to assure effective co-ordination of flow. The integrated divisions were usually defined by the market they served, since the demands of the different markets so profoundly affected the decisions involved in the co-ordination of flow. The executives in the general office, relieved of day-to-day operating decisions, were to concentrate on appraising the performance of the different divisions and determining the present and future allocation of the company's resources.

The new decentralized structure had become fairly well known and understood by the end of the thirties. Chemical firms, including Hercules, Monsanto, and to some extent Union Carbide, had adopted it before World War II. Westinghouse began to move toward a decentralized structure in 1934 and General Electric in 1939. In both giant electric companies the move came initially because of the difficulty of controlling the flow of consumer durables. United States Rubber and Goodrich both applied the Du Pont principles in the late twenties, while General Motors had a similar organization after the Du Pont-supervised reorganization of 1921. International Harvester, explicitly following the General Motors model, made the changes during the war, while Ford and Chrysler did the same immediately afterwards.

In the postwar years the strategy of diversification spread quickly to other less technologically oriented industries. Swift, National Dairy, Procter and Gamble, and other corporations in food and consumer perishables followed the earlier example of General Foods and General Mills. In time even the steel and aluminum companies started to develop new products. In nearly every case these firms also turned to the decentralized structure. By the nineteen fifties diversification and decentralization had become the compelling fashion in American industry.

In the years since World War II American corporations have widely accepted the organizational innovations and the operational procedures worked out before 1940 by the pioneers in modern corporate management. These same postwar years have been ones of impressive growth for the national economy and of rapid expansion for the industrial corporations. They have been years of economic stability as well as growth for the economy and for the corporations. The direct relationship between the spread of the new administrative forms and procedures and economic and corporate growth and stability would be difficult to define with any precision. Yet let me suggest some possible connections.

By complementing the policies and procedures developed in the federal government by the Council of Economic Advisers, by the Treasury, and by the Federal Reserve Board, the new controls over inventory and working capital may have helped to even out the business cycle and to make business fluctuations less severe and less dangerous than they have been in any other period of American history.

Certainly the institutionalizing of industrial innovation has been vitally significant to the continued growth of the economy and the corporation. And nothing has contributed more to the systematizing of such innovation than the increased use of the research laboratory in American industry and the adoption of the decentralized administrative structure. The research department of a corporation develops and tests the commercial value of a new product or process. The executives in the general office, free from routine activities, decide, on the basis of detailed information provided by their staff and by the divisions, whether to produce and market the product or process. If its production and distribution makes full use of the firm's existing resources, it will be manufactured and sold through an existing division. If it uses similar production facilities but requires quite different distributive ones, or vice versa—that is, if it can use existing distributing facilities but requires new production ones—then a new division can be formed. If its output employs very few of the company's existing resources, then the senior executives can decide to lease its manufacture and sale to another company. Moreover, the institutionalizing of product or process innovation has been concentrated more in producers' goods than in consumers' goods industries. The products of the chemical and electronics industries are purchased by customers not because of their style, comforts, or status-bringing qualities but because they cut the costs and improve the quality of their purchasers' own processes or products.

If competition encourages growth, the strategy of diversification and the decentralized structure have had an additional impact on postwar economic performance, for they have increased competition between large corporations. Compare the competitive situation in the old copper and the new plastics industries. In the copper industry, production and distribution are still dominated as they were forty years ago by the "big four." In the plastics business, most of the large firms in the technologically advanced industries are competing with one another. Not only do nearly all the large chemical electrical, rubber, and petroleum companies have plastics divisions but General Foods, General Mills, Borden, and Swift do as well. Within the past few months even United States Steel has moved into the competition. Where four giants produce by far the largest share of the nation's copper, ten times that many industrial giants are in the plastics business.

Although the direct connection between organizational and administrative innovation and economic growth cannot be precisely defined, it seems safe to say that the constant efforts which I have been describing to cut the costs of production and distribution, to assure a smooth flow of goods from the suppliers of raw materials to the final customer, to allocate economic resources rationally, and to develop and apply new processes and products systematically have been and continue to be essential to the health and growth of the American economy. By innovating in these areas, the corporation has surely played a major role in making the American economy the most productive in the world.

On the other hand, the overwhelming dominance of the large corporation in the modern American economy has raised problems and issues, some of which are still totally unresolved. The extreme concentration of power in a society committed to democratic values is one such issue. Another is the difficulty, if not the impossibility, of the corporation's allocating resources to meet socially desirable needs which bring only a low rate of return on investment. However, the first step in meeting these problems is the understanding of how the corporation developed the basic functions it has long enjoyed in the management of the American economy. Such an understanding is essential if the nation is to achieve the full promise of a consumer-oriented mass production, mass distribution economy operating within an open society.

IV
THE RISE OF AMERICAN MILITARY POWER

by Theodore Ropp

This paper begins in the eighteen eighties, when the United States was becoming the world's greatest industrial power. Its subsequent rise to military paramountcy—at a speed comparable to that of Rome in the third century B.C. or of the Hapsburgs in the sixteenth century—is, of course, a major feature of recent world history. The whole process has received some excellent interpretations, but only for particular wars.[1] Since there is none as yet for the entire story, this sketch will consider it in three thirty-year generations from the arbitrary bench mark of 1945 in terms of (1) the political and economic infrastructure of this military power, (2) changes in military technology, and (3) military institutions and concepts. While these last reflect the society of which the soldier is a part and which furnishes him the tools of his trade, one must also remember that he has a "mind" and institutions of his own and that these are as distinctive as the conformations of the professional politician, businessman, or scholar.[2] While our thirty-year generation is still incomplete, such a fixed time grid can be a corrective to a traditional historical periodization which is not procrustean enough, but which does show the importance of wars as datable and cataclysmic social events by following them

[1] One of the best is Kent Roberts Greenfield's *American Strategy in World War II: A Reconsideration* (Baltimore: The Johns Hopkins Press, 1963).

[2] The standard work on militarism is Alfred Vagts's *A History of Militarism: Romance and Realities of a Profession* (New York: W. W. Norton & Company, Inc., 1937; rev. ed., Meridian Books, Inc., 1959). Lt. Gen. Sir John Winthrop Hackett, *The Profession of Arms* (London: The Times Publishing Co., Ltd., 1962), is a modern classic.

too closely.[3] And, at least in modern times, this fixed grid can also be seen in terms of alternating periods of military normalcy and revolution. These periods seem analogous to those found—though not in any generational pattern—by Thomas S. Kuhn in the history of scientific development.[4]

Professor Kuhn sees "normal science as puzzle-solving" within an accepted paradigm or model. Anomalies then build up to "revolutions as changes of world view." The first tests of such anomalies are:

> trials only of themselves, not of the rules of the game. They are possible only so long as the paradigm itself is taken for granted. Therefore, paradigm-testing occurs only after persistent failure to solve a noteworthy puzzle has given rise to crisis. And even then it occurs only after the sense of crisis has evoked an alternative candidate for paradigm. In the sciences the testing situation never consists, as puzzle-solving does, simply in the comparison of a single paradigm with nature. Instead, testing occurs as part of the competition between two rival paradigms for the allegiance of the scientific community. . . . The proponents of competing paradigms are always at least slightly at cross-purposes. Neither side will grant all the non-empirical assumptions. . . .
>
> Since new paradigms are born from old ones, they ordinarily incorporate much of the vocabulary and apparatus, both conceptual and manipulative, that the traditional paradigm had previously employed. But they seldom employ these borrowed elements in quite the traditional way. Within the new paradigm, old terms, concepts, and experiments fall into new relationships.[5]

The great physicist Max Planck noted that "a new scientific truth does not triumph by convincing its opponents . . . but rather because its opponents eventually die, and a new generation grows up that is familiar with it."[6] Although Kuhn does not think that scientific revolutions follow any specific generational pattern, his model of scientific revolutions does seem useful in considering military

[3] The chronological bench marks in Robert R. Palmer and Joel Colton's *A History of the Modern World* (3d ed.; New York: Alfred A. Knopf, Inc., 1965) are all related to wars or treaties. Biological generations are not constant, but are still estimated at about thirty years, a span that Herodotus took from the Egyptians.

[4] *The Structure of Scientific Revolutions* (Chicago: The University of Chicago Press, 1962; Phoenix ed., 1964).

[5] *Ibid.*, pp. 144, 147, 148.

[6] Quoted by Kuhn, *The Structure of Scientific Revolutions,* p. 150.

changes. Quincy Wright and Lewis F. Richardson note forty- to sixty-year military cycles, which may be related to economic recovery from war or to what Wright calls "the waning social resistance to a new war as social memory of the last one fades with the passage of [its] generation."[7]

On a thirty-year grid, there is evidence of paradigm conflict in the generations 1766–95, 1826–55, 1886–1915, and that since 1945. In the first, 1766–95, theorists like Comte de Guibert outlined the "puzzles" for Napoleon. In the second, 1826–55, Karl von Clausewitz and the Prussian general staff saw some of the elements of total war in "the participation of the people in this great affair of state."[8] In the wars of national unification, 1856–85, both the Americans and the Prussians found out how to raise, train, command, move, and supply mass armies by rail and water, and they began to face the tactical problems of the Industrial Revolution's new weapons. Although presidential elections have trained Americans to think in short four- or five-year cycles—Wright's "usual life of a political administration in most countries and the average duration of a war between great powers"[9]—American history can be "fitted" into alternating generations: paradigm conflict, 1766—95; puzzle solving, from Washington's second administration through those of James Monroe, 1796–1825; conflict over the rules of the game, from John Quincy Adams through Franklin Pierce, 1826–55; and solutions for those puzzles that the people decided it was most important to have solved, from James Buchanan through Chester A. Arthur, 1856–85.

[7] *A Study of War* (2 vols.; Chicago: The University of Chigago Press, 1942; Phoenix ed., 1965), Phoenix ed., p. 344. After suggesting this pattern, neither Wright nor Lewis Fry Richardson, in his *Statistics of Deadly Quarrels,* ed. Quincy Wright and C. C. Lienau (Pittsburgh: Boxwood Press, 1960), studied it in detail. In many civilizations childhood ends at, say, fifteen; political apprenticeship may continue to, say, forty-five; and political decisions are made by older men. One might study this pattern by comparing the ages at which men were expected to reach the highest commands. A related problem is the life expectancy of weapons, which for nineteenth-century battleships was twenty years.

[8] Karl von Clausewitz, *On War,* tr. O. J. M. Jolles (New York: Random House, Inc., 1943), p. 543. In many ways his contemporary Baron Henri Jomini belonged to an earlier generation. See Theodore Ropp, *War in the Modern World* (2d rev. ed.; New York: Collier Books, 1962), pp. 150–60.

[9] *Study of War,* pp. 343–44.

This analysis of recent American military history deals with three arbitrary generations. From 1886 to 1915, the United States faced the problems of world power in an era of paradigm conflict, even in such "military" matters as the effect of the new fire weapons. Not surprisingly, the American debates on these issues were basically derivative and continued to be so during the generation 1916–45, but these debates brilliantly solved the European-set puzzles of two total wars. The contemporary generation, here defined as that since 1945, is again one of paradigm conflict, but Americans now lead the debate. No one can say that they are asking the "right" questions, but they are questioning some basic concepts of the generation of total war in a new technological and political environment. The resulting paradigm will use some of the ideas and much of the language of the generation in which the United States became the world's paramount power; it will have to be explained to the people who now determine these "great affairs of state." As the Italian theorist Giulio Douhet wrote a generation ago, "We shall glance at the war of the past long enough to retrace its essential features; we shall ask of the present what it is preparing for the future; and, finally, we shall try to decide what modifications will be made . . . by the causes at work to-day."[10]

The United States Looking Outward, 1886–1915

The political, economic, and ideological currents of this generation of imperialism had their American protagonists and opponents, but their arguments were derivative. On the place of power in international politics, the most original American works were the psychologist William James's "The Moral Equivalent of War"[11] and the anti-imperialist polemics of William Graham Sumner. James represented the pacifist current in American thought. Sumner feared the

[10] *The Command of the Air,* tr. Dino Ferrari (London: Faber and Faber, Ltd., 1943), p. 120.

[11] Published in 1910; reprinted in *War: Studies from Psychology, Sociology, Anthropology,* ed. Leon Bramson and George W. Goethals (New York: Basic Books, Inc., 1964), pp. 21–31.

state's increasing power over individuals; peace through armaments was a fallacy: "To pursue such a notion would absorb all the resources and activity of the state; this the great European states are now proving by experiment."[12]

Walter Lippmann has written that Theodore Roosevelt had seen "the elements of a genuine foreign policy," but had "sought to develop" it and the elements of American power —our strategic position, armaments, and alliances—without making them plain to the nation; that in this and the next generation, "the United States never made a sustained and prudent, or remotely adequate, effort to bring its obligations and its power into balance"; and that William Howard Taft and Woodrow Wilson "were idealists who habitually rejected the premises of the politics of power," disliked armaments, and abhorred alliances, but "favored a League of Nations in which the United States assumed the obligation to enforce peace."[13] The turn-of-the-century debates on the interests of businessmen, missionaries, or other expansionists laid down few guidelines for strategy. As William L. Neumann noted of the most controversial area of American strategy: "At no time in [this or] the interwar period did any responsible government official make a public and explicit statement of the priorities of American interests in Asia, the relationship of these interests to [other] American interests, . . . and which interests in Asia, if any, were vital enough to justify war in their behalf."[14]

American industry could furnish whatever weapons Congress would buy. American inventors—Sir Hiram Maxim, Bradley A. Fiske, Simon Lake, and the Wright brothers—contributed to the general development of weapons, but the services' adoption of such weapons was often slower than in Europe, a situation analogous to Great Britain's similarly

[12] "War" published in 1911; reprinted in Bramson and Goethals (pp. 205–27), pp. 226–27.

[13] *U.S. Foreign Policy: Shield of the Republic* (New York: Pocket Books, Inc., 1943), pp. 21–23.

[14] "Ambiguity and Ambivalence in Ideas of National Interest in Asia," in *Isolation and Security: Ideas and Interests in Twentieth-Century American Foreign Policy*, ed. Alexander DeConde (Durham, N.C.: Duke University Press, 1957), p. 140.

slow adoption of new weapons when she led the world in technology in Clausewitz's generation. New weapons were more quickly adopted by the United States and British navies than by their armies, whose roles remained primarily defensive or "colonial." The classic American "invention" first adopted by European armies was the airplane, but the United States Army was equally slow to adopt the automobile and new European explosives, such as smokeless powder. In spite and because of American industrial development in this and the next generation, Americans also underestimated the time required to turn their industrial and scientific potential into actual weapons.

The most influential American military theorists of this era were Emory Upton and Alfred Thayer Mahan. Upton committed suicide in 1881, and his *Military Policy of the United States*[15] was not published until 1904. Although he failed to show why the United States needed more military power, he argued that a larger regular army, backed by volunteers officered by regulars, would be cheaper and more effective than the traditional regular-militia combination. But Upton's slanted history and his attack on civilian control, which made his proposals for a general staff and a better system of higher military education sound more "Prussian" than they were, increased political resistance to his proposals. With the French writer Ardant du Picq and the German Klemens Meckel,[16] Upton saw the importance of individual training and more open order, but he failed to realize the defensive power of the weapons developed late in the nineteenth century. Upton thought that the dangers of the line's being penetrated were greater than those of its being outflanked and thought "the German method of

[15] Washington, D.C.: U.S. Government Printing Office, 1904. For his career, see Stephen E. Ambrose, *Upton and the Army* (Baton Rouge, La.: Louisiana State University Press, 1964).

[16] Ardant du Picq, *Battle Studies,* tr. John N. Greely and Robert C. Cotton (Harrisburg, Pa.: Military Service Publishing Co., 1958). Du Picq was killed in 1870, and his work was not influential until it was republished in 1878. On Meckel's influence in Japan, see Ernst L. Presseisen, *Before Aggression: Europeans Prepare the Japanese Army* (Tucson, Ariz.: University of Arizona Press, for the Association for Asian Studies, 1965), chs. III, V.

flowing around the flanks of strong points a mistake."[17] But Upton was an astute observer, and his *Armies of Asia and Europe*[18] remains one of the best surveys of its period. Partly because a similar "Prussianism" was being preached by many British army reformers, Americans took little interest in the European army, whose functions most closely resembled their own, and this view has held for the British army's role in "westernization" almost to the present day. The greatest British theorist of this era, G. F. R. Henderson, was far better known as the biographer of Stonewall Jackson than for his thoughts on volunteers or amphibious operations.[19] The army's attitude toward British experience was in striking contrast to that of the navy or the later air force.[20]

A. T. Mahan's *The Influence of Sea Power upon History, 1660–1783*[21] is one of the most influential books ever written by an American. A year younger than Upton, Mahan lived on until 1914, as "a pioneering geopolitical thinker . . . who touched off a whole series of attempts to explain the dynamics of world power."[22] Although it is hard to determine Mahan's influence on the actual course of the Anglo-German naval race or on the development of navalism, he provided a "do-it-yourself kit" for naval and world power.[23] He did not understand the technical arguments for the dreadnought, but he saw the importance of the command of the sea, of a battle fleet to fight for it, and of the many tactical

[17] Quoted by Ambrose, *Upton and the Army*, p. 63.

[18] New York: D. Appleton & Co., 1878.

[19] *The Science of War*, ed. Neill Malcolm (London: Longmans, Green and Co., Ltd., 1905).

[20] The standard work is Jay Luvaas, *The Education of an Army: British Military Thought, 1815–1940* (Chicago: The University of Chicago Press, 1964).

[21] Boston: Little, Brown and Company, 1890.

[22] Robert Brent, "Mahan—Mariner or Misfit?" *U.S. Naval Inst. Proc.*, XCII, No. 4 (April, 1966), 92–103; a fine study of Mahan's realization that "the acceptance of his ideas . . . was to some extent dependent upon his professional sea-going reputation in the navy of his day" (p. 92).

[23] See D. M. Schurman, *The Education of a Navy: The Development of British Naval Strategy Thought, 1867–1914* (London: Cassell and Company, Ltd., 1965), p. 71. On "updating" Mahan, see Clark G. Reynolds, "Sea Power in the Twentieth Century," *The Royal United Service Institution Journal*, CXI, No. 642 (May, 1966), 132–39.

problems of the close blockade and the defensive-offensive. His world reputation stemmed from his acceptance of current views of international politics, race, trade, and colonies; his formula for national greatness was to put all these isms together.

Mahan's faults were those of his age. It is hard to see how any American could have pumped for colonization when millions of Europeans were colonizing America's cities, or how anyone in that generation of industrial development could have regarded a large seafaring population as essential to a navy. But the world's greatest land power, with its model of a general staff, built the world's second navy without a clear idea of how it was to be used and did not even ask it to support that right wing that was vital to Alfred von Schlieffen's plan to envelop the French army. That the United States Navy could measure itself as a defender of the Monroe Doctrine against a High Seas Fleet built for the North Sea is not surprising. Mahan's *Naval Strategy: Compared and Contrasted with the Principles and Practice of Military Operations on Land*[24] said little about amphibious planning; the 1915 Gallipoli operation was visualized rather than planned. And C. E. Callwell's *Military Operations and Maritime Preponderance: Their Relations and Interdependence*[25] was, like his *Small Wars,*[26] published and forgotten. The United States thus accepted some of the cloudy European concepts of national power, built the world's third navy, and quadrupled its army. While the Bull Moose's nationalism was almost as flamboyant as that of William II, Elihu Root was astute enough to see that his army reforms could not be too Uptonian, and some of Mahan's neomercantilist nostrums were simply ignored in practice.

Administrative reorganizations usually stem from drives for economy or from breakdowns of the existing systems. Both the United States and the British army systems broke down in their first big overseas enterprises of this generation,

[24] Boston: Little, Brown and Company, 1911.

[25] Edinburgh: William Blackwood & Sons, Ltd., 1905.

[26] First published, 1898 (2d ed.; London: War Office, Her Majesty's Stationery Office, 1903).

Cuba and South Africa. The American system was described, in 1880, by a former chief of the navy's Bureau of Engineering: "A civilian . . . has supreme authority in naval affairs, and all questions of importance are decided by him. To assist in the administration there are eight Bureaus, the chiefs of which are naval officers, each having independent authority pertaining to the Bureau he controls."[27] The War Department had ten bureaus and a commanding general in 1898. The "general staff" of 1813 was no more than the bureau chiefs, who fought for their bureau interests. Congress had rejected a bill, which Upton had supported, for combining the Inspector General's and the Adjutant General's departments into a real planning body.[28] A Board of Navy Commissioners modeled on the Board of Admiralty had lasted only from 1815 to 1842.

A Naval War Board was set up in 1898. Its civilian member was the Assistant Secretary of the Navy, Theodore Roosevelt, and Mahan was called from retirement to serve on it. President William McKinley assumed active command, set up headquarters in his office, presided over strategy discussions with the secretaries and the bureau chiefs, and often revised orders and instructions to commanders in the field.[29] But the success of the Naval War Board and the General Board during Roosevelt's presidency gradually turned it from what Mahan called "embodied policy"[30] to shipbuilding programs, which Sir Thomas Brassey[31] called "the most difficult by far" of all the problems of naval administration. Brassey had been Civil Lord and Secretary to the Admiralty. He devoted three of the five volumes of his

[27] J. W. King, *The Warships and Navies of the World* (Boston: A. Williams and Company, 1880), p. 381.

[28] See Ambrose, *Upton and the Army,* pp. 116–18. The best general account is Russell F. Weigley's *Towards an American Army: Military Thought from Washington to Marshall* (New York: Columbia University Press, 1962).

[29] See T. Harry Williams, *Americans at War: The Development of the American Military System* (Baton Rouge, La.: Louisiana State University Press, 1960), p. 99.

[30] *Naval Administration and Warfare: Some General Principles, with Other Essays* (Boston: Little, Brown and Company, 1908), p. 84.

[31] *The British Navy: Its Strength, Resources, and Administration* (5 vols.; London: Longmans, Green and Co., Ltd., 1882–83), III, p. 2.

British Navy to hardware, one to the merchant marine, and one to administration.

On these management problems, European experience is significant. Sir John Fisher's success in getting the Royal Navy "ready" to face the Germans in the North Sea also inhibited detailed staff planning. His assistant, later Admiral Sir Herbert Richmond, wrote that Fisher would "neither seek nor accept counsel," that he would generalize about war, but that "a logical & scientific system of war is a different matter."[32] In February, 1915, just before Gallipoli, Richmond observed that "Fisher does nothing, Winston proposes mad things, Wilson opposes all suggestions made by anyone except himself."[33]

The "logical & scientific" procedures of a general staff, militia reforms, and the abolition of the post of commander-in-chief were imposed on the United States and British armies by two lawyers, Elihu Root and Lord Haldane of Cloan. Root was not a philosopher, but much of Haldane's epitaph would also apply to him: "A great servant of the state who devoted his life to the advancement and application of knowledge. Through his work in fashioning her army he rendered invaluable aid to his country."[34] Root became Secretary of War in 1899. He heard firsthand accounts of what had gone wrong and of the general staff systems in Germany and France; he read Spenser Wilkinson and found and published Upton's *Military Policy*. Although Root's system did not incorporate the best European practices or the American military experience of the past, it did result in an improved officer corps and more effective coordination at some higher levels of command.[35]

[32] Quoted by Arthur J. Marder, *Portrait of an Admiral: The Life and Papers of Sir Herbert Richmond* (London: Jonathan Cape, Ltd., 1952), p. 49.

[33] *Ibid.*, p. 140. The Wilson mentioned is Admiral Sir A. K. Wilson, at that time First Sea Lord.

[34] Quoted by Dudley Sommer, *Haldane of Cloan: His Life and Times, 1856–1928* (London: George Allen and Unwin, Ltd., 1960), p. 425.

[35] See Williams, *Americans at War*, pp. 100–1, 104–5, 124, and 115. The American postwar investigation was headed by a railway engineer, Representative from Iowa and Civil War Major General Grenville M. Dodge.

Interservice planning remained rudimentary in both countries. The 1911 army-navy quarrel that resulted in Churchill's appointment as First Lord of the Admiralty did not lead, as Richmond noted four years later,[36] to detailed strategic planning. If the Americans had not "come to grips with the immense problems of modern war,"[37] Europeans were equally unprepared for the deadlock that followed the Marne battle. The men whose fears were voiced by the Polish-Jewish economist and banker Jean de Bloch's *The Future of War in Its Technical, Economic, and Political Relations*[38] had been silenced. The technical sign of the end of war, Bloch thought, was the magazine rifle, which now made war and any decisive victory politically impossible. But most military men foresaw political victory—through the cloudy aphorisms of Clausewitzian and Social Darwinist nationalism—in a tactical victory, in a battle in which, so Marshal Ferdinand Foch wrote in 1903, armies would be hurled "*as one whole* on *one* objective."[39] This concept of victory was not further analyzed by anyone preparing for "this new sort of war, more and more national, . . . more and more powerful, . . . more and more impassioned; a war which does away with all systems founded on positive quantities: ground, position, armament, supply."[40] Such dogmas typified this age of paradigm conflict, one in which

---

Viscount Esher was the leading figure in the later British investigation of the Boer War.

On Spenser Wilkinson, see Luvaas, *Education of an Army*, pp. 253–90. His most famous work was *The Brain of an Army: A Popular Account of the German General Staff* (first published, 1890; new ed., with letters from Count Moltke and Lord Roberts; London: Constable and Company, Ltd., 1913).

[36] See Marder, *Portrait of an Admiral*, pp. 141–42.

[37] See Williams, *Americans at War*, p. 115.

[38] First published in 7 vols., St. Petersburg, 1898; vol. VI, tr. R. C. Long, intro. Edwin D. Mead and W. T. Stead (Boston: Ginn and Company, 1903); see esp. pp. xvi–xvii, xlix, and 355–56. Mead correctly felt that no other "book written in the cause of the peace and order of the world, save Hugo Grotius's, . . . has rendered or is likely to render such influential practical service."

[39] Ferdinand Foch, *The Principles of War*, tr. Hilaire Belloc (London: Chapman & Hall, Ltd., 1921), p. 47.

[40] *Ibid.*, p. 41.

American students of war and world politics made few theoretical contributions.

The United States and Total War, 1916–45

The story of this generation of total war is well known. Many puzzles set by the previous generation were solved. But the debates over collective security were couched in terms that went back to Bloch and the First Hague Conference, and at San Francisco in 1945 no one asked whether a restored Wilsonian League was really what was needed. The New Deal was progressivism writ in detail. In foreign policy the United States ruthlessly used its massive economic and technological resources for Wilsonian political ends.

Measurements were already in "megas." In both world wars a large proportion of American production went for the transportation of men and explosives overseas. Expanded industry and transportation then supported massive economic and political reconstruction. We can note parenthetically that Bloch's fear of the revolutions that would follow czarist Russia's defeat in a European war was not balanced by any vision of the ways in which the revolutionists might use Russia's economic potential for their programs of reconstruction and industrial development. Many of the first efforts to measure national potentials in food, manpower, industry, shipping, and gold came out of World War I. The related idea of measuring the Gross National Product came out of the planning for recovery from the depression. The first measurements were for economies under siege. Directed investment for particular war products was less noticeable to the public than the wartime socialism of rationing, conscription, and propaganda. Only later in this generation was it feasible for neo-Clausewitzians and neo-Marxists to ship whole populations to new industrial or disposal areas or to incinerate them *in situ* from the air. But the idea of such governmental action was one consequence of the nineteenth-century emphasis on "the participation of the people in this great affair of state."

The principles of technological and scientific mobilization for war were most clearly formulated by the industrial powers most vulnerable to blockade and counterblockade, Germany and Great Britain. They were applied with the greatest effectiveness by the United States to an economy with more fat, greater security, and consequently greater flexibility. The relation of weapons production to that power's economic, scientific, and technological resources is symbolized by the one guess and the "hard facts" of one weapons system.[41] In 1945, the United States was thought to have from three fifths to three quarters of the world's industrial plant. It had just built and used bombs with an estimated power of twenty thousand tons of TNT. That standard came from World War I. In his 1919 Rede Lecture, "Science and War," Lord Moulton, the Liberal mathematician, chemist, patent lawyer, and judge—who had charmed William II at a luncheon with Haldane in 1911, and who became one of Great Britain's Walter Rathenaus—discussed "what Science can do when it takes in hand a purely military subject," before turning to "cases in which War has appropriated discoveries not made directly for its purposes."[42]

The 1945 bomb, General H. H. Arnold claimed, could be mass-produced and delivered for $1,240,000, six times more economically than conventional bombs, and "with relatively unimportant exceptions all of the centers of civilization in the northern hemisphere are within reach of destruction at the hands of any major nation in that hemisphere."[43] Bloch's argument had now been reversed. Air power had become too cheap. Interestingly enough, the first formulas for what was now called Operations Research had been developed in World War I for aircraft performance by the British engineer F. W. Lanchester.[44]

[41] The scope of the best work on this subject is indicated by its subtitle: Irving B. Holley, Jr., *Ideas and Weapons: Exploitation of the Aerial Weapon by the United States during World War I, a Study in the Relationships of Technical Advance, Military Doctrine, and the Development of Weapons* (New Haven, Conn.: Yale University Press, 1953).

[42] Cambridge: Cambridge University Press, 1919, p. 16. Moulton was in charge of explosives production. The luncheon story is in Sommer, *Haldane*, p. 243. Rathenau, son of the Jewish head of the German electrical combine, was in charge of German raw materials procurement.

[43] "Air Force in the Atomic Age," in *One World or None*, ed. Dexter Masters and Katharine Way (New York: McGraw-Hill, Inc., 1946), p. 27.

[44] *Aircraft in Warfare: The Dawn of the Fourth Arm* (New York: D. Appleton & Co., 1917).

The most original military theorists of this generation were an Italian and a Chinese—Giulio Douhet and Mao Tse-tung. Douhet found the solution to the puzzle of military mobility in air power. The armies had functioned "as organs of *indirect* attrition of national resistance," the navies "as organs to *accelerate or retard* this attrition," and the air arm had tended to destroy nations "*directly*."[45] Like the Polish Bloch, the Italian Douhet underestimated the solidarity of the developed industrial powers. As Charles de Gaulle later noted, "The Great War was a revelation. . . . For generations universal suffrage, compulsory education, the equality of rights and obligations had combined to mould the nation into a single whole. . . . The mass movements and mechanization to which men and women were subjected by modern life had preconditioned them for . . . the war of peoples."[46] Douhet's insistence that an air force had to win the command of the air by battle and that it had to be an independent service paralleled Mahan's ideas; whether these parallels were deliberate has not been studied. Lord Trenchard had come to similar conclusions, and his influence was much greater in the United States, although a translation of parts of Douhet's book was circulated in the nineteen thirties. General William Mitchell was the chief protagonist of Lord Trenchard's doctrines.[47]

Sir Herbert Richmond and the French Admiral Raoul Castex were the most important naval writers of this generation. Castex raised more basic issues, but his work was almost unknown in the United States.[48] Neither writer had much to do with the United States Navy's development of carrier and amphibious forces. German submarine "tonnage" warfare and the "wolf-pack" technique came from their

[45] Douhet, *Command of the Air,* p. 152.

[46] *France and Her Army,* tr. F. L. Dash (London: Hutchinson & Co., Ltd., 1941), p. 50.

[47] See Andrew Boyle, *Trenchard* (New York: W. W. Norton & Company, Inc., 1962), and Thomas H. Greer, *The Development of Air Doctrine in the Army Air Arm, 1917–1941* (Montgomery, Ala.: Maxwell A. F. Base, Air University, 1955).

[48] See Schurman, *Education of a Navy,* pp. 110–46, and R. Castex, *Théories stratégiques* (5 vols.; Paris: Société d'Editions Géographiques, Maritimes et Coloniales, 1930–37).

World War I experience. American submarine doctrine and techniques for the very different conditions of the Pacific were developed independently.[49] The theory of armored warfare was developed by the British strategists J. F. C. Fuller and B. H. Liddell Hart, whose works were widely read in the United States, if only because, like G. F. R. Henderson, they saw "signposts that were missed" in the American Civil War. Liddell Hart's insistence on the "indirect approach" became part of the vocabulary of many American writers on strategy.[50]

Mao Tse-tung's brilliant theoretical adaptations of Clausewitz and Lenin to Chinese conditions were almost unknown in the West, although some of his techniques were described by Evans F. Carlson.[51] Robert B. McClure remarked that Joseph W. Stilwell's "experience in China convinced him that the only way to achieve the objective was through extensive reorganization not only of the *Chinese Army,* but of the *National Government* as well."[52] Clausewitz would have added that one could not revitalize either without reorganizing the people.

American military men of this generation were empirical synthesizers. The same thing could be said of Napoleon or of the officers around Lincoln or Bismarck. However, the Prussian idea that the modern Great Captain is the collective brain of a general staff had now been adopted by the United States Army. In World War II, the United States had to make major strategic decisions. Greenfield has shown that most of these decisions were sound and that while political elements could be found in most of them, military objectives

[49] See Jeter A. Isely and Philip A. Crowl, *The U.S. Marines and Amphibious War: Its Theory and Practice in the Pacific* (Princeton, N.J.: Princeton University Press, 1951).

[50] See Luvaas, *Education of an Army,* pp. 325–424, and B. H. Liddell Hart, *Strategy: The Indirect Approach* (London: Faber and Faber, 1954). Most "characteristic" of Fuller's many works is *The Conduct of War: A Study of the Impact of the French, Industrial, and Russian Revolutions on War and Its Conduct* (New Brunswick, N.J.: Rutgers University Press, 1961).

[51] *The Chinese Army: Its Organization and Military Efficiency* (New York: Institute of Pacific Relations, 1940).

[52] Quoted by F. F. Liu, *A Military History of Modern China, 1924–1949* (Princeton, N.J.: Princeton University Press, 1956), p. 180.

consistently prevailed, "because given the aim of inflicting total defeat on a powerful combination of enemies, strictly military considerations seemed, and probably were, the only ground on which a coalition with disparate political interests could be held together until that ambitious aim was achieved. . . . The strategic direction of World War II by the Allies is a classic model of military effectiveness in achieving the arduous aim that the architects of their strategy set for themselves."[53]

The only real differences between the Americans and the British—if we remember how often the British used the Americans to draw the Jovian bolts of their strategically amateurish chief—stemmed from British misunderstanding of the capabilities and the limits of American production, which required target dates long in advance in order to ensure delivery to all the theaters of a widely scattered war.[54] World War I had been fought only in Europe and the Near East. When North Atlantic convoys took up to two months to turn around, even transport provisioning had often seemed insuperable. The Russians never understood these complexities or why, to quote Earl F. Ziemke, their Allies had to overprepare their "amphibious invasion, a one-shot, do-or-die undertaking that afforded no latitude for preliminary sparring."[55]

Perhaps the most significant feature of this war was the way in which "strategic air war as the offensive par excellence had been the inspiration and goal of the pioneers and leaders of air power, British and American."[56] It had been both experimental and costly. A thousand-plane raid assembled the equivalent of an infantry division, squad by squad, to fly in formation to a distant target, to fight its way back, and to land with its dead and wounded. The target-

[53] *American Strategy*, p. 23.

[54] *Ibid.*, pp. 45–46. The historical effects of Churchill's epic *The Second World War* (6 vols.; Boston: Houghton Mifflin Company, 1948–53) must still be evaluated.

[55] "The German Defeat in the East, 1942–45," *Military Rev.*, XLV, No. 5 (May, 1965), 38. See also Dwight D. Eisenhower, *Crusade in Europe* (Garden City, N.Y.: Doubleday & Company, Inc., 1948), pp. 42–48, 222.

[56] Greenfield, *American Strategy*, p. 121.

ing and utility of these raids remain disputed, but it may be noted that the moral issues of area bombing had been acutely posed by the long-range guns of the mid-nineteenth century.[57] Just before his death in November, 1918, a British company commander, Wilfred Owen, saw "the people in England and France who thwarted a peaceable retirement of the enemy from these areas, . . . sacrificing aged French peasants and charming French children to our guns."[58] If Greenfield concludes that strategic bombing was "a bludgeon, producing its effect by cumulative weight, . . . rather than by a surgical operation," he also thinks that the use of air power by the Americans and British had a decisive effect on the war "and irreversible consequences for . . . strategy."[59] In this clear case of resistance to aggression, North Americans generally showed as little concern with the morality of massive retaliation as they did with the concentration camps for those Japanese who did not live in Hawaii, the only area seriously attacked.[60]

American military management was excellent. The split between the chief of staff and the A.E.F. commander in World War I was solved by merging the first post with that of the commanding general. Interallied, interservice, and civil-military production problems were solved by various *ad hoc* bodies, including an Office of Strategic Services with a cover name as odd as that for the World War I tank.

[57] In the nineteen thirties J. M. Spaight, *Air Power and the Cities* (London: Longmans, Green and Co., Ltd., 1930), argued that the air menace was only the naval bombardment "extended inland." The real problem was that no one before World War I had analyzed the effects of modern weapons on civilian populations.

[58] *The Collected Poems of Wilfred Owen,* ed. C. Day Lewis (New York: New Directions Publishing Corp., 1964), p. 177.

[59] *American Strategy,* p. 121. For the most authoritative study of World War II bombing, see Sir Charles Webster and Noble Frankland, *The Strategic Air Offensive against Germany* (vols. I–IV in *History of the Second World War, United Kingdom Military Series,* ed. J. R. M. Butler; London: Her Majesty's Stationery Office, 1961).

[60] See Stetson Conn, Rose C. Engelman, and Byron Fairchild, *Guarding the United States and Its Outposts* (in Office of the Chief of Military History, Department of the Army, *United States Army in World War II*; Washington, D.C.: U.S. Government Printing Office, 1964), chs. V, VIII. For the other problems of locating internal enemies by race, see p. 43. Foreign enemies could be located, of course, by map co-ordinates.

Although the British were often "shocked" at this American muddling through, T. Harry Williams feels that "all the great American leaders have been essentially improvisers. Improvisation, as Elihu Root forgot, is a part of the American national genius."[61] One wonders about the Manhattan Project.

American concepts of victory ran from Wilson's "the world must be made safe for democracy" to "unconditional surrender." These concepts were in line with the equally cloudy and messianic goals of contemporary nationalism and totalitarianism. The only peculiarly American thing about them was the idea that they might be attained in some written document or political structure at some relatively near point in time. And the conditions of *Victory through Air Power*—to use the title of a book by Alexander de Seversky[62]—had been set down by Douhet in 1921: "Command of the air means to be in a position to wield offensive power . . . complete protection of one's own country, the efficient operation of one's army and navy, and peace of mind to live and work in safety. In short, it means to be in a position *to win. To be defeated in the air* . . . [places one] at the mercy of the enemy, with no chance at all of defending oneself, compelled to accept whatever terms he [may] dictate."[63]

The Paramount Power, 1946–66

The contemporary generation is surely one of paradigm conflict. Attempts to define the American national purpose are themselves significant.[64] In the mid-sixties America's elders are constantly worried about their youngsters, perhaps

[61] *Americans at War,* p. 125. Edward M. Coffman, *The Hilt of the Sword: The Career of Peyton C. March* (Madison, Wis.: University of Wisconsin Press, 1966), points up the need for a scholarly biography of John J. Pershing.

[62] New York: Simon and Schuster, Inc., 1942, the original edition of his *Air Power: Key to Survival* (New York: Simon and Schuster, Inc., 1950).

[63] *Command of the Air,* p. 24.

[64] For amusing contemporary comments on this soul-searching, see Eric Larrabee, *The Self-Conscious Society* (Garden City, N.Y.: Doubleday & Company, Inc., 1960). For the key work, see U.S. President's Commission on National Goals, *Goals for Americans* (Englewood Cliffs, N.J.: Prentice-Hall, Inc., 1960).

because there are so many dependent adolescents and senior citizens, perhaps because so many "soft" youngsters are openly revolted by an education overtly justified in terms of national wealth and power. Whether the old truths have become too dogmatic or have been eroded by overexposure, by un-American ideas, or by the grindstones of the new technology is surely a significant historical puzzle.

Political paradigm conflicts appear most sharply in the two limited wars that have followed victory in the Pacific and East Asia. However the political-military "Establishment" (a significant new term for the United States) manages these debates, it produces only an "operators' " consensus against the groups at the ends of the political spectrum. Each group accuses the others of losing touch with "reality." That European political slogans seem equally unpalatable to many of their youngsters reinforces this impression of paradigm conflict. Much of the debate is over lost opportunities; much of it turns on the idea that both wars have been partly caused by the failure of Great Britain and the United States to clarify their interests and commitments and to make it equally clear that they will fight to uphold them against both direct and indirect aggression.

Much of the American debate ignores the history of the Industrial Revolution. The Americans, Germans, Japanese, and Russians have already shown how developing national states with major resources can upset the industrial and military balance of power under a wide variety of "modern" ideologies. Like some German "realists" in the nineteen twenties, some new American realists claim that no power can dominate the others very long or make the world safe for any ideology. The German-educated political scientist Hans J. Morgenthau, whose *Politics among Nations* is the standard postwar American text on "interest defined in terms of power,"[65] and Walter Lippmann, the "realistic" critic of Wilsonianism, both oppose the Vietnam war. Lippmann thinks that the Administration has become separated "from the best brains of the country" and from the realities of the modern world and that in treating Vietnam as "another

[65] New York: Alfred Knopf, Inc., 1948, p. 5.

Appalachia," it is compounding the political costs of "three centuries of white imperialism and colonialism."[66]

The *deus ex machina* is technology. The world revolution of rising expectations has partly come from the shotgun unions of science and philosophy. The historian William H. McNeill holds that the "accelerating self-transformation" that he sees in modern European history will, "with the recent institutionalization of deliberate innovation in the form of industrial research laboratories, universities, military general staffs, and planning commissions," make "an accelerating pace of technical and social change" persistent and normal. Even non-Westerners, he thinks, can win "worldwide political-military authority . . . by utilizing such originally Western traits as industrialism, science, and . . . one or other of the democratic political faiths."[67] The deliberate merger of science and philosophy makes it even harder to separate political-economic issues from those of military technology, concepts, and management, and, finally, from the basic issues of "victory," and how it can best be managed.

The bench marks of this paradigm-conflict generation are "datable" inventions, wars, crises, debates, and, since the United States is the paramount industrial-military power, what have been its two-term presidencies. The Truman years saw demobilization in 1946, the beginning of the Cold War, Titoism, and service unification in 1947, an air force-navy row in 1948, Russian atomic tests, Mao's victory in China in 1949, and the Korean War. The Eisenhower years were marked by the development of American, Russian, and British thermonuclear and tactical atomic weapons, French nuclear tests, ballistic missiles, space vehicles, and nuclear submarines for firing missiles from under water. The 1953–55 "summit" accords went with alliance cementing and "massive retaliation." They were followed by the Suez and Hungarian crises and further service unification in an era of "nuclear plenty." The Kennedy-Johnson administrations saw the development of "flexible response," intelligence

[66] *The Atlanta Constitution* (April 28 and 30, 1966).

[67] *The Rise of the West: A History of the Human Community* (Chicago: The University of Chicago Press, 1963), pp. 567, 806–7.

satellites, and antimissile missiles. The Cuban and Berlin crises, Sino-Indian war, and Sino-Soviet split of 1961–62 were followed by the limited nuclear test ban and the "hot-line" of 1963. The Cyprus and Dominican crises, Chinese nuclear tests, and Indian and Vietnam wars of 1964–65 added to a list of conflicts that would surely make American policy makers agree with Leon Trotsky's note that anyone wanting a quiet life should not have picked this century.[68]

Much political debate, as has been noted, has dealt with the familiar issues of imperialism, isolation, collective security, and economic cycles. The Eisenhower years saw what the economist Calvin B. Hoover terms "the conservative acquiescence in the changed American economic system."[69] By 1956, both parties had "acquiesced" in large peacetime armaments expenditures. Such armaments had not, to recall William Graham Sumner's warning, absorbed "all the resources and activity of the state."[70] Eisenhower notes that, in contrast to 1954, his chairman of the Council of Economic Advisers had reported to "a relaxed, though receptive, audience." He adds that "the amount or absence of tension in a Cabinet meeting often mirrors the condition of the nation's economy."[71] But by 1960, an alleged "missile gap" and economic "stagnation" were key political issues. While the "missile gap," like many arms comparisons, turned out to be nonexistent, the "stagnation" charge marked the change from the Keynesian puzzles of economic stability to those of total national economic and military development in an era of "competitive co-existence."

[68] Richardson's *Statistics of Deadly Quarrels* should be updated, but the first problem would be to get a list of such quarrels. In an address to the American Society of Newspaper Editors in Montreal, Secretary of Defense Robert S. McNamara claimed that "in the last eight years alone there have been no less than 164 internationally significant outbreaks of violence," involving 82 governments; only 15 had been "military conflicts between two states, and not a single one . . . has been a formally declared war" (*New York Times* [May 19, 1966], p. 11). His criteria of significance were not stated.

[69] *The Economy, Liberty, and the State* (New York: Twentieth Century Fund, 1959; Anchor Books, 1961), ch. IX.

[70] See above, n. 12.

[71] *Mandate for Change, 1953–1956* (Garden City, N.Y.: Doubleday & Company, Inc., 1963; New American Library, 1965), p. 580.

The stagnation issue was dramatized by a 1960 RAND report, *The Economics of Defense in the Nuclear Age,* by Charles J. Hitch and Roland N. McKean. "All *military* problems," they argue, involve "economic problems in the efficient allocation and use of resources."[72] They discuss the resources available for defense, resource limitations, the size of the Defense Budget, and the shift from wartime shortages, with long-term investments deferred to peacetime, to the sustained peacetime arms program. They say that the most important of the indirect effects of defense spending is probably the spillover from military research and development and that the Russians are getting more because they devote a much greater proportion of their scientific and technical resources to military work. A series of tables, on a 1950–56 base, show that the Gross National Product of the major powers will increase until 1975 at the following annual rates: U.S., 2.5–3.5 per cent; England and France, 2–3 per cent; Italy, 3–4 per cent; West Germany and Japan, 4–5 per cent; and U.S.S.R., 5–6 per cent. When these rates were compounded on the assumption that totalitarian Russia could put more of its peacetime budget into arms, it seemed clear that she might outstrip the free nations in building military forces and upset the balance of terror. The Soviet Union's top peacetime military spending level was 10 per cent. By putting 15 per cent of its more rapidly growing GNP into arms, Russia might match the United States by 1965. "The smaller powers . . . will not (with the probable exception of China) produce major military capabilities even by 1975."[73]

The historian W. K. Hancock's fear that the Americans might "throw in their hand before the Russians" came from the belief that Americans would not accept the controls necessary for "a high rate both of industrial growth and of defence expenditure."[74] By 1966, the Russians were adopting some American methods, and John K. Galbraith was doubt-

[72] Cambridge, Mass.: Harvard University Press, 1960; New York: Atheneum Publishers, 1965, p. v.

[73] *Ibid.,* pp. 88–89.

[74] *Four Studies of War and Peace in This Century* (Cambridge: Cambridge University Press, 1961), pp. 29–30. Hancock was one of the editors of the British War Histories.

ing America's ability to support the Great Society's internal and foreign policies. In the previous paradigm-conflict generation, it might be noted, it was a German geographer, Friedrich Rätzel, who topped Mahan in proclaiming that sea power meant world power, while it was the British geographer Halford MacKinder who founded geopolitics on "The Geographical Pivot of History" in the Eurasian "heartland."[75]

Contemporary historians are usually right after the fact. It is now easy to see that these analyses ignore such factors as the military effectiveness of such cheap weapons as the Stone Age poisoned stake. If Hitch and McKean are alarmed by the Americans' tendency to underestimate Soviet achievements, even fewer are aware of the handcrafted adaptations of Western weapons by such "primitives" as the American Indians, the Maoris, or the Zulus, although this is not related to their equal ignorance of how advanced biochemical weapons may be developed and hidden by minor industrial powers. This is, in turn, directly related to a major strategical development, the deterrent or blackmail power, not only of second-rate nuclear, but also of fifth-rate scientific, states.[76] Hoover stresses the power of liberty in peace as well as in war,[77] but Hancock is less sanguine about the Americans' ability to "manage" liberty in a peacetime arms race.[78]

A final factor, more directly related to the economic limits of military power, is the possibility that, while the new econometrics might bring sustained economic development, military research, if only because it developed earlier, might be in an era of diminishing returns. In the American economic system, as Jerome B. Wiesner has noted, profit encourages experimentation—"Where individual initiative can-

[75] See Ropp, *War in the Modern World*, pp. 298–300.

[76] *Ibid.*, p. 396. Many of these handcrafted adaptations by "civilized" but "underdeveloped" peoples are not considered in the best book on the subject, Henry Holbert Turney-High's *Primitive War: Its Practice and Concepts* (Columbia, S.C.: University of South Carolina Press, 1949).

[77] *Economy, Liberty, and the State*, p. 404.

[78] See above, n. 74.

not respond, . . . the feedback process performs less well."[79] Though, to quote Hancock again, "wars which we prepare for but do not fight, wars which we fight but do not prepare for, . . . all have to be paid for,"[80] cost does not offer continuous comparisons with military reality.

The most significant weapons developments of this generation have already been mentioned. The powers loaded themselves with lethal "agents" and "delivery" systems, though "proliferation" usually meant the number of nuclear powers, rather than the number and variety of their nuclear, biological, and chemical agents, some of whose non-lethal forms presented major health hazards. An American decision to try to reverse air power's development by mass producing antimissile missiles and civil defense structures was put off by their cost, by the expense of the Vietnam war, and, basically, by the increasing sense of security that stems from Russian moderation, the Sino-Soviet split, the massive retaliatory power of missiles in hardened silos and hidden submarines, and the effectiveness of spy satellites in detecting the major ground force concentrations that would now have to precede any attack on the strong NATO forces. There were real virtues in systems that gave both sides time to think and that made it possible to return to the old legal requirement of warning before use of any weapon that would cause mass civilian casualties. The weapons "balances" struck annually by budget makers and politicians went back to the early industrial era and to Brassey's *Naval Annual* of 1886. The "missile gap" myth suggests that current examples of this art form are little better than the British and German ship and head counts for the "two-power" standards of Brassey's era. "An enemy's powers of resistance," Clausewitz noted, may be "expressed as a product of two inseparable

[79] "Society as a Learning Machine," in *The Computer and Society: Six Viewpoints* (*New York Times*: American Federation of Information Processing Societies, XI, April 24, 1966), p. 15. A Presidential Scientific Adviser was as significant an addition to the bureaucracy as the Council of Economic Advisers. Walt W. Rostow, *The Stages of Economic Growth: A Non-Communist Manifesto* (Cambridge: Cambridge University Press, 1960), failed to suggest a possible plateau in weapons development.

[80] *Four Studies,* p. 18.

factors: *the extent of the means at his disposal* and *the strength of his will.*" The former is "capable of estimation, as it rests (though not entirely) on figures, but strength of the will is much less so and only approximately to be measured by . . . the motive behind it."[81]

Military concepts are now so linked with military and political management practices that few generalizations can be made about the jungle of military literature. The air power underbrush is dead, and some of its trees are dying. We cannot say that this era has a Bloch or Mahan, but Admiral Henry E. Eccles' *Military Concepts and Philosophy*[82] is a sturdy second-growth survey of basic principles and new technologies. The Anglo-American wartime unity of aims and concepts remains reflected in important British works on strategy, but the increasing imbalance of that alliance is also reflected in the much greater volume and variety of American military research and writing.

This American paramountcy is most marked in the applied social sciences. While Hitch and McKean were using systems analysis in military economics, the Michigan economist Kenneth E. Boulding based his *Conflict and Defense: A General Theory*[83] on the British mathematician Lewis F. Richardson's models of *Arms and Insecurity*,[84] published

[81] *On War*, p. 6. For a recent work on nuclear proliferation, see Leonard Beaton, *Must the Bomb Spread?* (London: Penguin Books, for the Institute for Strategic Studies, 1966). There have been no studies of biochemical proliferation. On the state of this art, see Carl A. Larson, "Biological Warfare, Model 1967," *Military Rev.*, XLVI, No. 5 (May, 1966), 31–39; on nonlethal chemicals, see "Pandora's Box," *The Scientific American*, CCXIV, No. 4 (April, 1966), 49–50; on civil defense see my "Civil Defense Problems in the Great Lakes," *Sixth Seminar on Canadian-American Relations* (Windsor, Ont.: University of Windsor, 1965), pp. 149–54. See also Louis Morton, "The Anti-Ballistic Missile: Some Political and Strategic Considerations," *Virginia Quart. Rev.*, XLIV, No. 1 (Winter, 1966), 28–42. The best balance sheets are by Alastair Buchan for the Institute for Strategic Studies; the most recent is his *Arms and Stability in Europe* (New York: Frederick A. Praeger, 1963).

[82] New Brunswick, N.J.: Rutgers University Press, 1965.

[83] New York: Harper & Brothers, for the Center for Research in Conflict Resolution at the University of Michigan, 1962.

[84] *Arms and Insecurity: A Mathematical Study of the Causes and Origins of War*, ed. Nicolas Rashevsky and Ernesto Trucco (Pittsburgh: Boxwood Press, 1960).

posthumously in the United States in 1960. Many of the games theorists who had founded *The Journal of Conflict Resolution* in 1957 agreed with Boulding "that the intellectual chassis of the broad movement for the abolition of war has not been adequate to support [its] powerful moral engine . . . and that [its] frequent breakdowns are due essentially to a deficiency in its social theory."[85] Although this was the age of the Edsel, and not all social scientists heeded the British physicist P. M. S. Blackett's warning that the utility of mathematical analysis falls with the complexity of the problem,[86] many works in the applied social sciences were increasingly sophisticated. The physicist Herman Kahn, to take a well-known example, followed the science fiction of his *On Thermonuclear Warfare* with a better titled *On Escalation: Metaphors and Scenarios*.[87] Some of the resulting jargon—"damage limitation," "extended deterrence," "civic action," and "stabilization operations"—indicated thought rather than the conceptual confusions of a paradigm-conflict generation in which principles and policies must be re-examined in a rapidly changing technological and political environment.

In such cases, military management may change rather slowly because future wars are so obscure. In the United States, where so many management techniques were developed, some were first applied in the interservice rows that reached a peak in 1948. If Samuel P. Huntington's *The Soldier and the State: The Theory and Practice of Civil-Military Relations* took a Utopian-Uptonian view of the "conservative realism of the professional military ethic,"[88] some soldiers of the late forties were as intemperate as the European soldiers of Bloch's generation.[89] This suggests two

[85] *Conflict and Defense,* p. vii.

[86] *Studies of War, Nuclear and Conventional* (Edinburgh: Oliver and Boyd, 1962), p. 198.

[87] *On Thermonuclear Warfare* (Princeton, N.J.: Princeton University Press, 1960); *On Escalation: Metaphors and Scenarios* (New York: Frederick A. Praeger, 1965).

[88] Cambridge, Mass.: Harvard University Press, 1957, ch. III.

[89] See Morris Janowitz, *The Professional Soldier* (Glencoe, Ill.: Free Press, 1960).

more generalizations. First, some key issues—particularly those of civil defense and the roles of conscripts and reservists in an era of increasing professionalization—were blacked out. Second, the failure to agree on professional issues forced civilians into some of those very matters on which they were *a priori* least competent. War was already "repoliticized," but the soldiers' declining role in military decision making, a trend that Huntington hoped to see checked, was also due to their intemperance—with nasty charges of "disloyalty" or "muzzling" and the use of "kept" civilian analysts and publicists. The age of the civilian "military intellectuals" had begun, though their major theoretical works did not appear for another decade.

The social scientists' neglect of conscription partly came from political factors, which made it either dormant or too hot to handle. Under the American nuclear umbrella, the NATO powers did not expand conscription. Britain gave it up in 1962; France's professionals were backed by the static militias proposed by Air Marshal Sir John Slessor in 1954.[90] The United States kept conscription in order to spur volunteering. The intake from the 1940 Selective Training and Service Act, ended except for its machinery in 1947 and revived almost unchanged in 1948, has depended on circumstances. Basic reforms, when it comes up for renewal, might lead to its abolition. Changing demographic and educational patterns increasingly throw its burdens, as Secretary McNamara has said, on "a minority"—an inequity that might be ended by asking everyone to serve for two years "in one of the military services, in the Peace Corps or in some other volunteer developmental work. . . . For it would underscore our whole purpose . . . anywhere in the world where coercion, or injustice, or lack of decent opportunity still holds

[90] *Strategy for the West* (New York: William Morrow and Company, Inc., 1954). See also Pierre Gallois, *The Balance of Terror: Strategy for the Nuclear Age,* tr. Richard Howard (Boston: Houghton Mifflin Company, 1961), and André Beaufré, *An Introduction to Strategy*. tr. E. H. Barry (New York: Frederick A. Praeger, 1965); both reflect De Gaulle's emphasis on professionalism. His *Army of the Future* (Philadelphia: J. B. Lippincott Company, 1941) was translated long before his more significant *Edge of the Sword,* tr. Gerard Hopkins (New York: Criterion Books, 1960).

sway."[91] But conscription will be examined partly on its military merits and partly, like Britain's adoption of it in 1939, to emphasize a particular foreign policy commitment.

Yet this is why the draft is under fire, whatever the merits of the "Peacenik" notion that conscripts could opt out of particular military theaters. Few Americans know that Canada and South Africa have tried this, that western European conscripts were not used in nineteenth-century colonial wars, or that this has made such wars more unpopular and more easily branded as "capitalistic."[92] Conscripts were sent to Malaya and Algeria in the nineteen fifties, but the conflict in Algeria seems more like the American war in Vietnam, where France did not use conscripts. In 1958, France had to choose between the myth of a French Algeria and her traditional boundaries and between the Algerian generals and Charles de Gaulle.[93] Many Americans never felt that Korea involved a total national interest, though North Korea was a direct aggressor. North Vietnam's aggression is less direct. That this enemy cannot reach the United States and that this forces its use of unconventional tactics make American nationalist, if not ideological, passions harder to arouse and has allowed the enemy to play on traditional American and United Nations' sympathies for the underdog, the underdeveloped anti-imperialists.

With politics, technology, and military concepts now so interrelated, it is useful, finally, to trace these generalities chronologically by administrations. The army, burdened with the job of occupation, was hardest hit in the almost mutinous great demobilization of 1946, a phenomenon as American as apple pie and as palatable to all parties. It could not meet General Albert C. Wedemeyer's call for

[91] *New York Times* (May 19, 1966) p. 11. William James and others have made similar proposals. The Civilian Conservation Corps was an approach to this idea; the same proposal was made and defeated in 1940.

[92] See Ropp, *War in the Modern World,* p. 265, and "Politics, Strategy, and the Commitments of a Middle Power," in *Canada-United States Treaty Relations,* ed. David R. Deener (Durham, N.C.: Duke University Press, for the Duke University Commonwealth-Studies Center, 1963), pp. 81–101.

[93] See John Stewart Ambler, *The French Army in Politics, 1945–1962* (Columbus, Ohio: Ohio State University Press, 1966).

troops in China; when the draft was revised in 1948, it had ten skeleton divisions.[94] The Cold War had begun in 1947, with the Truman Doctrine of March 12, Secretary of State George C. Marshall's European recovery proposals of June 5, and their theoretical justification in "The Sources of Soviet Conduct" in the July issue of *Foreign Affairs*. The anonymous author, the State Department specialist George F. Kennan, head of its new Policy Planning Staff, found Soviet diplomacy "at once easier and more difficult" to deal with than that of such aggressive leaders as Napoleon and Hitler; the Russians were more rational, but at the same time less easily discouraged. He proposed "a policy of firm containment" that would increase the internal strains in the Soviet system and promote "the break-up or the gradual mellowing of Soviet power. For no mystical, Messianic movement . . . can face frustration indefinitely without eventually adjusting itself to the logic of that state of affairs. . . . Providence, by providing the American people with this implacable challenge, has made [them] dependent on their . . . accepting the responsibilities of moral and political leadership that history plainly intended them to bear."[95]

The air force-navy row over the supercarrier, a marginal weapon against a power that could be contained from land bases, pushed the navy into developing the Polaris submarine. But for almost a decade the main American strategical force was to be the air force, and the main tactical force, the army. And this row and the far more significant shift in American foreign policy combined to obscure such postwar evaluations of military policy as those of the President's Advisory Commission on Universal Training, headed by Karl T. Compton, Vannevar Bush's *Modern Arms and Free Men: A Discussion of the Role of Science in Preserving Democracy*,[96] and the

[94] Liu's *Military History* (see above, n. 52) is as good as Lionel M. Chassin's dated *The Communist Conquest of China: A History of the Civil War, 1945–49*, tr. Timothy Osato and Louis Gelas (Cambridge, Mass.: Harvard University Press, 1966).

[95] "The Sources of Soviet Conduct," in Richard L. Watson, Jr., *The United States in the Contemporary World, 1945–1962* (New York: Free Press, 1965), pp. 62–64.

[96] New York: Simon and Schuster, Inc., 1949.

Strategic Bombing Survey.[97] This survey is the best example of the civilian-military analyses (J. K. Galbraith headed its Overall Economic Effects Division) that were prepared by the wartime Air Force Office for Operations Analysis and later institutionalized by the private RAND Corporation. RAND, whose first charter was prepared for the Chief of Air Staff for Research and Development (RAND), General Curtis LeMay, was to study the methods, techniques, and instrumentalities involved in the formulation of air force plans, policies, and programs. If its first studies reflected the interests of the aircraft industry, RAND was the first of what Gene M. Lyons and Louis Morton call the new American "schools for strategy."[98]

These postwar works all reflect the primacy of air power and the "absolute weapon."[99] The Compton Commission[100] listed the essentials of an integrated national security program: (1) a strong, healthy, educated population, (2) a coordinated intelligence service, (3) scientific research and development, (4) industrial mobilization and stock-piling, (5) regular armed forces (with the interesting subheads: striking air force; army, navy, air forces, and marines; unity of command), and (6) universal training.

The Commission reported on May 29, 1947. The so-called "do-nothing" Eightieth Congress omitted universal training from the 1948 Selective Service Act, but it accepted a Central Intelligence Agency, research and development, the Munitions Boards, and the Joint Chiefs of Staff, Joint Staff, National Security Council, and Defense Department

[97] The 208 European and 108 Pacific War Reports of the United States Strategic Bombing Survey are listed in its *Index to Records of the United States Strategic Bombing Survey* (Washington, D.C.: U.S. Government Printing Office, 1947).

[98] *Schools for Strategy: Education and Research in National Security Affairs* (New York: Frederick A. Praeger, 1965), esp. pp. 246–47.

[99] *The Absolute Weapon: Atomic Power and World Order,* ed. Bernard Brodie (New York: Harcourt, Brace & Co., 1946). Brodie moved from Yale and the newly formed National War College to RAND. His *Strategy in the Missile Age* (Princeton, N.J.: Princeton University Press, 1959) is still one of the best works on the subject.

[100] *A Program for National Security: Report of the President's Advisory Commission on Universal Training* (Washington, D.C.: U.S. Government Printing Office, 1947), esp. pp. iii, 12–16.

in the National Security Act of 1947. Secretary of Defense James Forrestal forced the Key West "Roles and Missions" treaty of 1948. The Secretary of Defense got the power to direct and control (not co-ordinate) the "military" departments in 1949.[101]

These managerial problems were then blanketed by Korea (when the marines won a seat on the Joint Chiefs, and which resulted in a Defense Supply Management Agency in 1952), the economic and military needs of the NATO and other containment pacts, and the President's dismissal of General Douglas MacArthur. With all the American ground forces in Korea, except the two divisions in Germany, western Europe was defended by the striking Air Force. In this crisis the Joint Chiefs, as their Chairman, General Omar N. Bradley, noted at the MacArthur hearings on May 15, 1951, unanimously agreed, since Red China was not seeking to dominate the world, to oppose expanding "the wrong war, at the wrong place, at the wrong time, and with the wrong enemy" and to choose "the basic objective of the American people—as much peace as we can gain without appeasement."[102] General Eisenhower, then Supreme Commander in Europe, saw Truman's right to remove MacArthur as "unchallengeable."[103] The best prospects in Korea, he thought, were for an eventual stalemate, since the United States would not repeat Hiroshima. When he became President, he settled for "an armistice on a single battlefield,"[104] because the Soviets also had a quantity of atomic weapons.

Eisenhower stressed the horizontal or functional analysis of available defenses. The Secretary of Defense was given more authority in 1953 and the power to consolidate, transfer, or reassign service functions in 1958, when the Joint Chiefs became a "command post" for the Unified and Speci-

[101] See Robert P. Beebe, "The Vital Key West Agreement," *U.S. Naval Inst. Proc.*, CXVI, No. 9 (Sept., 1961), 35–41; and Paul Y. Hammond, *Organizing for Defense: The American Military Establishment in the Twentieth Century* (Princeton, N.J.: Princeton University Press, 1961).

[102] Quoted in Watson, *United States in the Contemporary World*, pp. 120–21, 123.

[103] *Mandate for Change*, p. 39.

[104] *Ibid.*, p. 230.

fied Commands. Emphasis was then on the reallocation of resources—improved nuclear weapons, better means of delivery, and effective air defense. Service rivalries were transferred to the Joint Chiefs. The President kept out of these military disputes, where an army officer's intervention would surely have been resented. A 1961 study[105] found the services ready for joint action. The most important remaining issues were those of further unification and a single Chief of Staff.

The present Defense Department organization dates from Eisenhower's last two Defense Secretaries and especially from Thomas S. Gates, Jr. When the U-2 and Bay of Pigs disasters showed some slippage between the services and other executive agencies, the Kennedy-Johnson administrations tightened the White House controls. The historian Stanley L. Falk studied the role of the National Security Council;[106] that of the White House Staff awaits the scrutiny of the political scientist McGeorge Bundy.

No one has studied the styles of Louis A. Johnson, Truman's second Defense Secretary, or Eisenhower's Charles E. Wilson, but both held McNamara's view that the Secretary of Defense should not be "passive."[107] By the end of Eisenhower's second term, Congress had developed the habit of using service pressure groups to vote more money for air power and air defense, instead of cutting arms expenditures. Raymond H. Dawson and Samuel Huntington have studied this in some detail.[108] The Secretary of Defense eventually became chief foreign salesman for that "'military-industrial complex" against whose "unwarranted influence" Eisenhower

[105] Albert T. Church, Jr., and Lloyd R. Vasey, "Defense Organization Issues," *U.S. Naval Inst. Proc.*, LXXXVII, No. 2 (Feb., 1961), 23–30.

[106] "The National Security Council under Truman, Eisenhower, and Kennedy," *Political Science Quart.*, LXXIX, No. 3 (Sept., 1964), 403–44.

[107] "McNamara Defines His Job," *New York Times Magazine* (April 26, 1964).

[108] Raymond H. Dawson, "Congressional Innovation and Intervention in Defense Policy: Legislative Authorization of Weapons Systems," *Am. Political Science Rev.*, LVI, No. 1 (March, 1962), 42–57; and Samuel P. Huntington, "Interservice Competition and the Political Roles of the Armed Services," in *Total War and Cold War: Problems in Civilian Control of the Military*, ed. Harry L. Coles (Columbus, Ohio: Ohio State University Press, 1962), pp. 178–210.

warned in his farewell address,[109] but no postwar president has bought enough air power to satisfy Congress. Since it cannot compel presidents to spend more money, some of these have been sham battles, but, like those during the European arms races of the late nineteenth century, they often made American policy seem more militant and more capitalistic.

The Swiss theorist Urs Schwarz has seen this American "military-scientific-industrial community" as both consumer and producer of ideas: if "the natural scientist and the national economist have frequently been over-rated," and "the military has submitted too readily to . . . civil analysts, leadership, face to face with the electronic brain, has not abdicated."[110]

About the "new warfare," which began with the Korean War, the first in which air power was shackled, Brigadier C. N. Barclay,[111] the editor of the *British Army Quarterly,* commented that now communism and democracy are about evenly matched, physically, and that the present high cost of total armament is ruining both groups. He said that "new" or cold war now involves propaganda, underground war, sabotage, intimidation and bribes, war by proxy on a limited scale, the armed threat, obstruction, and planned mischief.

Although Garibaldian and Marxist techniques of national and social liberation have been winning wars for centuries, the western powers seem unprepared for what Andrew M. Scott calls *The Revolution in Statecraft: Informal Penetration:* "National boundaries have become porous. Techniques have been fashioned to provide agents of one nation with direct access to the population and processes of another. . . . It provides new means of generating political

[109] "Farewell Radio and Television Address to the American People, Jan. 17, 1961," *Public Papers of the Presidents of the United States, Dwight D. Eisenhower, Jan. 1, 1960 to Jan. 20, 1961* (Washington, D.C.: U.S. Government Printing Office, 1961), pp. 1038–45.

[110] "The Development of U.S. Strategy: A Swiss View," *Military Rev.,* XLVI, No. 6 (June, 1966), 23–24. His *Strategy: Yesterday, Today, Tomorrow* is forthcoming.

[111] *The New Warfare* (New York: Philosophical Library, 1954), esp. pp. 9–10, 16–18.

instability—and allows the development of techniques and institutions to achieve stability."[112] American and Russian adjustments to the new paradigm seem more thorough than those of the other powers. China, not Russia, still sees the "new warfare" as a panacea. The 1957 British White Paper stressed nuclear arms, professional forces, and an air-mobile Central Reserve; 1966 finds her main forces still tied to Germany and her Indian Ocean position still dependent on South African co-operation. The theoretical undating of De Gaulle's *Army of the Future* includes the impossible job of purging "massive retaliation" of its "Anglo-Saxonisms."[113]

"The only product of American strategic thought understood and subscribed to in Europe," Colonel Schwarz notes,[114] was massive retaliation in the "extreme and absolute form" of Dulles' speech on January 12, 1954. Eisenhower does not comment on Mr. Dulles' style, but notes their "substantial agreement."[115] The reliance upon strategic air power, John W. Spanier has commented,[116] appealed to the American people because it sounded more dynamic and was obviously cheaper than large balanced forces. Dulles himself had feared that the earlier policy of dependence on conventional weapons "could not be continued for long without grave budgetary, economic, and social consequences. . . . A great capacity to retaliate, instantly, . . . permits a selection of military means."[117] But events ended Eisenhower's hope that the United States would not need more ground forces and conventional weapons. Massive retaliatory power did damp some

[112] *The Revolution in Statecraft: Informal Penetration* (New York: Random House, Inc., 1965), pp. v, 175–76.

[113] See P. K. Kemp, "Editor's Notes," *Journal of the Royal United Service Institution*, CXI, No. 642 (May, 1966), 96–98; and Eugene Hinterhoff, "British Defense Review," *Military Rev.*, XLVI, No. 6 (June, 1966), 76–81.

[114] "U.S. Strategy," p. 26.

[115] *Mandate for Change*, p. 123.

[116] *American Foreign Policy since World War II* (2d rev. ed.; New York, Frederick A. Praeger, 1965), p. 106.

[117] In his earlier *War or Peace* (New York: The Macmillan Company, 1950), Dulles had realized that "it would not be possible in any predictable time to build up in Western Europe a military establishment . . . [of] any *offensive* significance. Indeed, it cannot have much *defensive* significance, except against indirect, internal aggression" (p. 119). He saw "no simple formula . . . and no single act that will assure peace" (p. 4).

conflicts, but it required better co-ordination, hot lines, and intelligence. McNamara's damage limitation" seems to imply that civilians would be spared in thermonuclear strikes on "military" targets;[118] hardened missile and hidden Polaris sites may increase the chances of bargaining with a "developed" state. Still trumpeting their weights, the superpowers have turned to the real problems of new kinds of warfare.[119] Both the United States and Russia, as Mao put it in 1957, have had to "let a hundred schools of thought contend" without upsetting "the correct handling of contradictions among the people."[120] With its atomic cannon an instant curiosity, the United States Army has had to think about the "new warfare." The problem for Special Forces, counterinsurgency, civic action, and so on, is how to defeat or contain an underdeveloped enemy who offers few targets to conventional forces, but can get specialized weapons from his allies or in the open market. These are the problems which have produced the most significant works of a period in which increasingly massive retaliatory and conventional forces have not yet fully checked indirect aggression.[121]

[118] See George E. Lowe, "Damage Limitation: A New Strategic Panacea?" *U.S. Naval Inst. Proc.*, XCI, No. 6 (June, 1965), 39–47.

[119] See *Military Strategy: Soviet Doctrine and Concepts*, ed. V. D. Sokolovsky (New York: Frederick A. Praeger, 1963). Sokolovsky was Chief of the General Staff from 1953 to 1960. "Strategic rocket troops . . . constitute the foundation of mass armed forces," but he admitted that nuclear weapons would have to be supplemented by "the most diverse military equipment" (pp. 225, 223). In this work, the western citations are as interesting as the lack of citations from nonwestern sources.

[120] *Mao Tse-tung: An Anthology of His Writings*, ed. Anne Fremantle (New York: Mentor Books, 1962), pp. 284, 264. This speech was delivered on February 27 and revised on July 1, 1957.

[121] The British White Paper (1957); the RAND reports of Brodie and of Hitch and McKean (see above, nn. 99 and 72); Henry A. Kissinger, *Nuclear Weapons and Foreign Policy* (New York: Harper & Brothers, for the Council on Foreign Relations, 1957), revised as *The Necessity for Choice: Prospects of American Foreign Policy* (New York: Harper & Brothers, 1961); *Prospect for America: The Rockefeller Panel Reports* (Garden City, N.Y.: Doubleday & Company, Inc., 1961); Fritz Sternberg, *The Military and Industrial Revolution of Our Time* (New York: Frederick A. Praeger, 1959); Thomas C. Schelling, *The Strategy of Conflict* (Cambridge, Mass.: Harvard University Press, 1960); James M. Gavin, *War and Peace in the Space Age* (New York: Harper & Brothers, 1958); and Maxwell D. Taylor, *The Uncertain Trumpet* (New York: Harper & Brothers, 1959).

When such indirect aggression was countered by more active American involvement in the defense of South Vietnam, the American conventional buildup was both massive and relatively rapid. The American forces were generally well trained. Spot equipment shortages were chiefly due to heavy dependence on air supply in an area with little ground transport and to a lack of local and light-draft shipping. Helicopters were known to be vulnerable and versatile; they have had to be used in spite of heavy losses. Heavy bombers were used for jobs for which they were not designed, and light bombers in conditions and against point defenses for which they had not been designed. Reserves were not called to do jobs they had been kept to do, but such political-military incongruities always occur and may be a special feature of wars in which a great power hopes for a quick end to bargaining with a small opponent. Many noncurrent problems—civil defense is the best example—have been blanketed, but Congress has strongly reasserted its role as adviser and educator on policy.

Some of the hundred blossoms of the years since 1957 have faded, but basic military issues have been studied more systematically than in any previous era in American history. Such studies have ended the separation of technological means and political ends that seemed practical only a generation ago. Revived eighteenth-century jargon may suggest that the "new warfare" is a professional sport, but it still involves the people. This is why Clausewitz would surely fear that miscalculation or the frustrations of either the professionals or the people might still overcome reason. Force remains important in international affairs, and no state has tried Commander Sir Stephen King-Hall's training for passive resistance.[122] The new paradigm that might be drawn

[122] *Power Politics in the Nuclear Age: A Policy for Britain* (London: Victor Gollancz, Ltd., 1962). Some of the post-Eisenhower "puzzle-solving" works have already been noted. Others that may be of major theoretical interest are: Inis L. Claude, Jr., *Power and International Relations* (New York: Random House, Inc., 1962); Thomas C. Schelling and Morton H. Halperin, *Strategy and Arms Control* (New York: Twentieth Century Fund, 1961); Morton H. Halperin, *Limited War in the Nuclear Age* (New York: John Wiley & Sons, Inc., 1963); and Glenn H. Snyder, *Deterrence and Defense: Toward a Theory of National Security* (Princeton, N.J.: Princeton University Press, 1961).

from these studies may be summarized as follows: (1) Military power still largely depends on the union of science, technology, and philosophy for political and economic policies. (2) Technology has now made nuclear war politically unacceptable, has limited conventional and unconventional war in Europe, and has unified the world conflict arena. (3) All military, political, and economic policies now have international repercussions. (4) Since the great industrial powers still control most of the world's capital, industry, markets, and transport, access to these assets is a major bargaining counter. (5) Since underdeveloped states are not strong enough to develop a stable international order, this remains a primary responsibility of the traditional great powers.

If total victory over a great power is now almost impossible, limited "winning" is possible only if the resulting bargain can be satisfactorily explained to the publics concerned. The difficulties of this feat are proportional to Clausewitz's "interests closely affecting the people."[123] Familiarity may condition them to see that messianic victories are unlikely; containment, permeability, coexistence, and the like are tags for the gradual weakening of the dogmas of total war and total victory.[124] Douglas MacArthur saw this dilemma quite clearly: "The scientific methods which have made mass destruction reach appalling proportions and the integration of the world have outlawed the basic concepts upon which war was used to settle international disputes," but "if one great power keeps armed and threatening, the only way you can meet force is by force, and you have to provide for it."[125]

One new soldier wrote recently, "As surely as the 'old Army' left its imprint on the officer corps, so too has the 'new Army' produced a new soldier. . . . War . . . is his job, not his inspiration. He accepts the concept of war

[123] Clausewitz, *On War,* p. 583. For Liddell Hart's hope that the powers would find that "mutual restraint is beneficial to self-interest in the long run," see *The Revolution in Warfare* (New Haven, Conn.: Yale University Press, 1947), pp. 109–19.

[124] See William L. Gordon, "What Do We Mean by 'Win'?" *Military Rev.,* XLVI, No. 6 (June, 1966), 3–11.

[125] Quoted in Ropp, *War in the Modern World,* p. 403.

without victory, but he does not really understand it. . . . In the absence of firm doctrine, he has become extremely flexible. . . . Indeed, he could be described, with[out] . . . irony, as a modern version of the traditional American 'citizen-soldier.' "[126] But much of this could be said, fortunately, of the great professional soldiers of the last generation.

[126] Dave R. Palmer, "The Return of the Citizen Soldier," unpublished paper (Duke University, May, 1966).

INDEX

INDEX

designer: Gerard Valerio
typesetter: Baltimore Type and Composition Corporation
typeface: Baskerville
printer: Universal Lithographers, Inc.
paper: Mohawk Tosca Book
binder: Maple Press
cover material: Spine, G.S.B. No. 95
Sides, Strathmore Grandee, blue